...eible
President and Chief Executive Officer

...ear Fellow Team M...

...his leadership meeting is dedicated to the
Power of You! It doesn't matter how many
corporate campaigns we create; without you to
power it, we will not succeed.

...hope you enjoy this book as I did. It is a
simple read. I did a lot of self-reflection.
I'm sure, like me, you will find some concepts
to apply to ATS and your personal life.
BE PRESENT! Join me, won't you?

PORT**BUTLER**
MEET AND GREET SERVICE

6.6.17

Sally

WINGTIPS
— YOUR TRAVEL LOUNGE —

More Praise for *Leading with Intention*

Leading with Intention should be required reading for any-one leading an organization or a team. It is a wakeup call to those who rely too much on the old adage 'Half of life is showing up.' The ideas in this book are powerful, providing concrete tools for successfully leading intentionally in all aspects of life."

—*Douglas J. Swirsky, President and CEO, GenVec, Inc.*

"Leading with Intention gives leaders a skillful way to examine and enhance their impact. A terrific gift for your-self and your team."

—*Jim Schoeneck, President and CEO, Depomed, Inc.*

"I have long awaited the publication of this book. Mindy's concepts—elegant in their simplicity and practical in their application—make this the go-to manual for leadership impact!"

—*Lisa Uthgenannt,*
Senior Vice President of Human Resources, Covance

"Leading with Intention will change the way you think and challenge you to be the best leader you can be. It is a valu-able addition to your leadership toolkit."

—*Margaret (Peggy) Coons,*
Senior Vice President of Human Resources,
Horizon Blue Cross Blue Shield of New Jersey

"Dr. Hall speaks from the heart and from twenty-five years of mindful professional experience. This book speaks in straightforward language to being a better person as well as a better leader. Not only is this an inspirational read, but it's a handbook that I will use regularly and share with my staff."

—*Joe V. Selby, MD, MPH, Executive Director, Patient-Centered Outcomes Research Institute*

"I have worked extensively with Mindy and believe that this book captures and distills many of her most important leadership principles into a quick read that will improve the function and success of any management team."

—*David Hung, MD, President and CEO, Medivation, Inc.*

"We all likely have a collection of how-to business books proudly displayed on our shelves. This one remains on my desk."

—*Jeffrey Keisling, Corporate Vice President, and Chief Information Officer, Pfizer*

"Leadership is critical to the success of any organization or team—and leadership behaviors can be learned. Dr. Hall's book provides down-to-earth principles born out of real-world experience that will prove invaluable to those committed to learn."

—*Joseph Scodari, Worldwide Chairman, Pharmaceuticals, Johnson & Johnson (Retired)*

"Learning to lead with clear intention and understanding is something that each and every leader, regardless of experience or focus, can benefit from. This book is a worthy use of a leader's time."

—*Laurie Cowan, Senior Vice President of Human Resources, CSL Group*

LEADING WITH
INTENTION

LEADING WITH
INTENTION

Every Moment
Is a Choice

Mindy Hall, PhD

copper bay press

Copper Bay Press, LLC
6542A Lower York Rd., #135
New Hope, PA 18938
www.copperbaypress.com

Ordering Information
Quantity sales. Special discounts are available on quantity purchases by corporations, associations, and others. For details, contact the "Special Sales Department" at the address above.

Printed in the United States of America

Cataloging-in-Publication Data

Hall, Mindy, 1963–
     Leading with intention : every moment is a choice /
Mindy Hall, PhD.—First edition
     pages cm
     Includes bibliographical references and index.
     LCCN 2014941803
     ISBN 978-1-941770-09-2

     1. Leadership. 2. Self-consciousness (Awareness)
     I. Title.

     HD57.7.H35 2014   658.4'092
     QBI14-600101

First Edition
18 17 16   10 9 8 7 6 5 4 3

For Marge, Rohinish, and Sue.

Thank you.

Contents

PART I—
MIRROR, MIRROR ON THE WALL:
Recognizing Your Impact

PART II—
ROME WAS NOT BUILT IN A DAY:
Leading with Intention Takes Practice

PART III—
A COMMUNICATIONS DEPARTMENT OF ONE:
Being Intentional in Your Communication

PART IV—
NO ONE WORKS ALONE:
Impacting Your Organization

PART V—
THE RIPPLE EFFECT:
Paying It Forward

Preface

∙∙

Every interaction is an opportunity.
Every action has an impact.
Every moment is a choice.
Are you choosing the impact you want to have?

In the late '80s, I walked into an auditorium filled with bright-eyed young professionals looking to make their mark on the world; we had been called together for what we thought was going to be a slide presentation by one of our most senior vice presidents. We settled in and assumed "reception mode" (we all know what that looks like—passive listening and sometimes not even listening) and prepared to hear an hour's worth of content. What happened next has never left me. The vice president leading the meeting walked to the front of the room, flipped the front page of a flip-chart pad over, and there, written on the paper were two words: "Be Here!" He didn't go into any depth about what was on the page but left it there the entire meeting as he talked through the latest developments of an acquisition the company was making.

It got me thinking: how many people were "there"? Who was "present"? Who was not? What choices were people making and what was the impact of those choices? These questions are at the heart of *Leading with Intention*, as I believe that every moment we have is a moment of choice: an opportunity to consciously decide how we will show up.

In my work with leaders across continents and organizations, I see a common thread. No matter what level of leader I am working with or what part of the world I am working in, once leaders begin to intentionally choose who they want to be and the impact they want to have, their effectiveness exponentially rises, both in their leadership and their lives. The most wonderful part of this fundamental truth is that this choice rests entirely with the individual; the power to show up any way you would like rests in your hands. Be here.

Introduction

....

Who do you want to be as a leader? What impact do you want to have? How do you want people to experience you? No matter where you fall in the organizational structure, your ability to shape both the organizational culture and how others perceive you is a direct result of the level of intention with which you operate. What does it mean to operate with intention? It is consciously deciding to lead by design rather than by default; being mindful of who it is you want to be and then living into that picture twenty-four hours a day. It is about seeing opportunities every day, in every interaction, to shape the tone, the experience, and the outcome of those interactions. It is realizing that the system you work in does not tell you who you get to be; you decide who you get to be.

In any given moment—in your professional life and in your personal life—you have the ability to get the results you want and to have the impact you want. Every interaction provides that opportunity; every moment is a choice. *Leading with Intention* was born of a belief that everything you do sends a message: what you say and how you say it, what you do and how you do it, even what you choose not to say or do. Seeing your "self" as the primary tool for achieving high-level results is a concept that may seem like common sense, but it is far less commonly practiced and even less often developed in professionals as they grow in their careers.

Here's an example: a young professional, about three years out of a very prestigious MBA program, asked my opinion about a leadership topic while we were on a break at a meeting; as I began to answer her question, she pulled out her phone and started texting. When I paused, she stopped texting and looked up with a quizzical expression on her face as if to say, "Well, go on, I'm listening." After spending the next ten minutes talking to her about the unintentional impact of her behavior, namely that my response to her question had been seemingly ignored, it was as if a light bulb had gone on. She began to see, in a whole new way, that what she was choosing to do out of habit was not positioning her in the way she wanted to be perceived. When she decided to share her learning with others in the meeting, they all commented on how useful they thought it would be to develop this way of thinking more explicitly in leaders: to teach them the concept of how to lead with intention, how to make conscious choices about their impact on others, how to use themselves more profoundly, and how to integrate this mind-set into their way of viewing themselves and the world. Imagine the impact if this sort of learning was not the exception but the rule.

This book is not a quick fix but the beginning of an evolution. It is meant to be read in one or two sittings but thought about and used over a lifetime. It asks you to make your growth personal. Indeed, many of its concepts get to the core of who you want to be as a person, as a leader, as a contributor to your organization, and as a citizen of the world. It provides concrete ideas that can be applied immediately and contains stories and real-life examples (though all names have been changed to maintain anonymity). *Leading with Intention* draws on my experience over the past two decades of unlocking capacity in individuals and organizations to create extraordinary business results. And while the concept of using oneself has not traditionally been on the business radar screen, its time is long overdue in the hallways of our organizations as it makes a profound difference in the leader you can be and the results you can achieve.

Parts I and II of this book focus primarily on the individual in relationship to the topic of intention—increasing your awareness and building the concept of intention into your leadership and your life. Part III looks at communication, one of the most tangible ways in which intention is made visible. Part IV targets the intersection of the individual with the organization—how everyday interactions affect the bottom line and how one person can shape organizational culture. Finally, part V asks you to consider how to pay it forward—how you can become a pebble in the pond, moving this kind of thinking beyond yourself and your organization and out into the world.

Lofty in its aspiration but real in its potential, *Leading with Intention* promotes a grand vision: the use of self as a way to improve your life, your relationships, your leadership, your organization, and the world. For those who see the advantages of leading with intention—both the tangible rewards of building a successful organization and the emotional rewards of creating an environment that inspires—the chapters that follow provide a road map. Those who have done this work will tell you that it's a greater journey than they ever imagined. I encourage you to make a difference, to make a choice to use yourself more intentionally, to be a catalyst for unleashing capacity and potential in others, and to know that once you begin walking this path, nothing will ever be the same. Let's get started.

MIRROR, MIRROR ON THE WALL
Recognizing Your Impact

Your ability to lead with intention is built upon a foundation of awareness—of your intentions, your mindsets, your impact on others, and your organizational context. Without awareness, you simply won't have the data you need to make intentional choices about your behavior.

Part I encourages you to recognize and take responsibility for the impact you have on the people and environment around you.

He who knows others is wise.
He who knows himself is enlightened.

LAO-TZU

CHAPTER 1

Leading with Intention

Intention, as defined by Webster's, is "a determination to act in a certain way." While simple in concept, intention can be quite difficult in practice. The conscious, deliberate element here is what proves to be elusive for most of us as we rush through our days meeting deadlines, picking up children, attending meetings, and trying to find the balance among it all. Who has time to think about "who they are being while they are being"? I say, "Who can afford not to?" So much of what happens in the course of a day is the result of unchallenged patterns that have worked for us in the past: out of intuition, not intention; out of reaction versus conscious choice. Paying attention to who you are being is certainly not an easy path; it takes energy and hard work to be deliberate about how you will engage in each interaction. But the benefit for you and those around you is worth the effort. While awareness is the foundation, what you do with that awareness is what counts. It does little good to have the knowledge and not use it.

In my executive coaching work, I focus my efforts around three layers of growth (fig. 1.1):

- The *awareness layer* lies at the core of growth: it is about cognition, sparking the brain to pay attention, and being able to see oneself with an objective eye—to "get it" intellectually.

- The *integration layer* takes that cognition and turns it into behavior; it is the leap from the cognitive to the behavioral that is the hardest to make and causes the most frustration. Think, for example, about declaring that you are going on a diet: while your brain may fire up with that goal in mind, you still may reach for a bag of M&M's before realizing, behaviorally, that you just ran counter to what your brain said you wanted to do. Or take the example of an executive who decides he wants to be more assertive in meetings, but then falls into an old pattern of passively listening more than actively contributing. We often experience a series of fits and starts before we actually hold true, behaviorally, to what we say we want to do.

- The *embodiment layer* is about consistency over time. So, the executive mentioned above who wants to be more assertive in meetings will only be able to make this shift if he operates in the new behavior consistently over time. Growth is a process, not an event; and just as developing the muscles needed to act in new ways takes time, cementing the shift takes time. Consistency has a compounding effect, and the more you behave in a specific way, the more likely the behavior will continue.

Any behavior change will go through some iteration of these steps, so as you begin to more consciously recognize

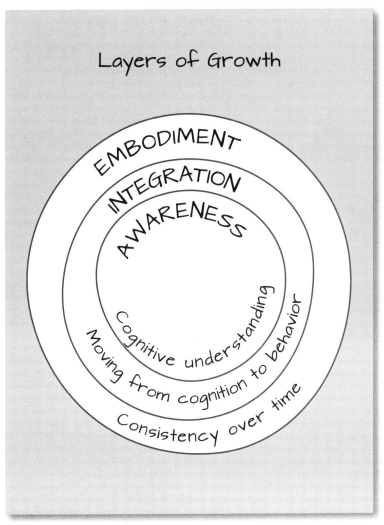

FIGURE 1.1 Layers of Growth

your impact, you will undoubtedly move through these layers of growth. In reality, people can learn to do things quite
quickly; it is the consistent integration of new behaviors
and attitudes that marks embodiment and true personal
growth. Changing programmed ways of operating takes
time. Be patient with yourself and with the process.

Challenge your patterns.

CHAPTER 2

Developing Self-Awareness

Recognizing your impact begins with self-awareness: an understanding and an ownership of the contribution you make to any dynamic. I once worked with the leadership team at a growing manufacturing company that had big issues to tackle—the divestiture of a division, outsourcing of some critical functions, and a large product launch on the horizon. Clearly, these were issues that would require the team to really pull together to be able to solve them. In our meetings, one executive was controlling the conversation, pushing for decisions before the rest of the team was finished vetting various ideas, and essentially shutting down the conversation. She got somewhat masked feedback about her behavior in the form of good-natured ribbing: comments like, "You better get your opinion in quickly or Kris will give your opinion for you" and "There's no need to talk about it; Kris already has the answer." While they spoke in a joking manner, the team was getting frustrated with how Kris was operating. So on one midmorning break, I gave her some direct feedback about how she was impacting the room. She responded, "Oh, I can't help it; I just happen to be intense," with no regard to her impact on the team. This was an excuse, not an end state. She knew how she was coming across yet felt no need to shift. Though she understood her contribution to the dynamic, she did not take ownership for it; until she was willing to do that, she would not be able to change it.

Sometimes the impact is subtler. Here's an illustration of this point on an organizational level. A vice president of human resources worked in a company where the corporate offices were set up with two entrances: the front door from the lobby, which visitors were encouraged to use, and a side entrance marked "Employees Only," which staff were *required* to use. The company's senior-most executives could use either door, and it was about the same distance from their parking spaces to their offices no matter which route they chose. Going through the side door took them past many offices and common areas, allowing them to interact with other people in the company. Many of the executives, however, used the front door of the building, as they felt it afforded them more expedient access to their offices and therefore made better use of their time. What they failed to realize, however, was the gap between their intent and their impact.

The perception the executives created among employees was that they thought of themselves as separate—that they didn't care to interact with the employees and did not have to follow the same rules. This behavior, although seemingly innocent, contributed to an "us-versus-them" feeling that began to impact the organization in very real ways—lack of belief in the espoused values of the company, lack of trust in the executives, and lack of engagement. Unintended consequences, but ones that illustrate how easily actions send messages and how small behaviors can have a tangible impact.

The common and powerful truth is that it all begins with a completely controllable variable: your awareness—awareness of self and personal impact, awareness of the context in which you are operating, and awareness of where self and organization intersect—of how you "show up" to those you are leading. If I asked those who work around you, those who work for you, and those for whom you work to describe how you "show up," what would they say? Are you shaping that picture intentionally or is it happening by default? People are watching: are you intentionally choosing your behavior or leaving its impact to chance?

How aware are you of how you're perceived?

CHAPTER 3

Noticing Yourself

My first job after college was running a nonprofit crisis center. I was on call 24/7. I spent a lot of time at police stations and hospitals. Most of the time I didn't pay much attention to my appearance. If I got a call in the middle of the night I would throw on a pair of jeans and a T-shirt and out the door I would go. Although I probably should have looked much more professional, I did not place much importance on the impact of my appearance.

A few years later, I took a job at a large, multinational bank where I was responsible for developing new leaders. When I started, a friend told me I needed to go out and spend some money on clothes. I had no money. I had an entry-level salary, rent to pay, a car payment and student loans, and I am fairly certain that I did not even have a credit card. Spending money on a new wardrobe seemed impractical to me. I told my friend that if the company didn't see me for the value I could bring—no matter what clothes I came in—it probably wasn't the right place for me. Looking back, I was either incredibly naive or incredibly arrogant. Here I was, a recent college graduate entering a new industry, and I expected a major, established corporation to accommodate my style. I thought, "They should not judge me based on my clothes; they should judge me for what I can contribute." Then my friend asked me one of the best questions I have ever been asked. She asked, "If you went on [an American] football field in a basketball uniform, how effective would you be in reaching your goal?" That analogy was an epiphany for me. She continued, "You have to get on the field to be able to affect the field. If you come on the field in a different uniform than is needed to play, you will never be able to affect the game the way you want to." She was right. I still had no money, but I decided that I wanted to be on the field; I decided I wanted to affect the field. So I went out and invested in new clothes. The clothes were simply the price of entry, but without them my ability to have the influence I wanted would have been compromised. That was when I began to understand the power of how one "shows up"—physically and emotionally.

In every interaction, you are the pivotal element. You have the ability to tailor your approach, your message, your actions—and even your appearance—to shape the outcome. You must, therefore, begin to see your self as the primary tool for achieving high-level results, as opposed to elements outside of you—such as business models, organizational structure, other people, or circumstances.

Over the course of my twenty-five-plus years coaching leaders and shaping organizations, I would say nearly 80 percent of those I have worked with did not lead intentionally. They were bright, capable leaders that operated out of intuition, pattern, and reaction. Mind you, some did so with very strong results, but those who made the decision to be more self-aware and intentional achieved higher-level results in terms of both the positions they've held and the impact they've had than those who continued to operate primarily from intuition.

Developing this aptitude is possible and begins the moment you look in the mirror and reflect on the process of understanding how you show up, how you affect a room, and what environment you create. Operating with this level of awareness is counterintuitive to how we live our lives, which is why it is so easy to lose sight of its importance. However, with this awareness in place, success becomes a matter of intention: recognizing who you are being and choosing consciously and deliberately who you want to be. Put more plainly: *notice yourself.* Be in the moment and watch yourself in the moment. How would you experience your actions if you were on the receiving end? Create a moment-to-moment awareness that allows you to pivot, shift, and adjust. While simple in theory, it requires tremendous self-discipline.

Most people lead through intuition, using patterns that have worked in the past, versus leading with great intention. Think about Mark Zuckerberg and the controversy that was sparked when he wore a hoodie on the stock exchange floor when Facebook was taken public. It started with a comment by Michael Pachter on *Bloomberg Television* where he stated, "Mark and his signature hoodie: He's actually showing investors he doesn't care that much; he's going to be him. I think that's a mark of immaturity. I think that he has to realize he's bringing investors in as a new constituency right now, and I think he's got to show them the respect that they deserve because he's asking them for their money." Others shot back with opposing views and quips, some with tongue-in-cheek sarcasm that spoke of disdain for Pachter's comments. Box CEO Aaron Levie pointed out on Twitter, "After Facebook hit $1B in profits, you'd think investors would start demanding Zuck wear a hoodie." He went on to say, "Yahoo CEO: No hoodie; AOL CEO: No hoodie; Facebook CEO: hoodie. Coincidence?"

No matter what your opinion is of the behavior, the bottom line is that it had an impact. For some, it signaled that he was "doing his own thing" and "not selling out to the establishment"; for others, it failed to inspire confidence that Zuckerberg could lead in the bold, new "post-IPO Facebook" world. The question is not so much whether he did the right thing wearing a hoodie but rather whether CEO Zuckerberg intentionally chose the impact he wanted to have.

You choose every day how you engage with the world around you. Don't waste that opportunity. Don't allow your life or your career to develop by chance; make those choices with intention. The question for you is what are you choosing?

Every action has an impact;
choose wisely the impact you want to have.

CHAPTER 4

Noticing Yourself Through Another's Eyes

Think back to a conversation you've had in which you felt you had the other person's undivided attention, you felt heard and paid attention to, you felt that what you had to say was valued. Nothing compares to that feeling of having someone 100 percent present with you, verbally and nonverbally. However, with the multitude of draws on our attention—texts chiming in, Twitter updates, e-mail notices, Facebook posts, and phones ringing—it is no wonder we feel challenged to stay present in the moment. The next time you have a conversation, notice how the level of your presence affects the tenor of the conversation. Notice yourself through others' eyes. What do they see?

My friend Mary's son is making his way up the corporate ladder as a sales leader. Hard driving, he sleeps four hours a night, can't sit still for more than fifteen minutes, and is tied to his smartphone. At Mary's home one Saturday evening for a small family gathering to celebrate her birthday, I noticed that as the family sat around the table together bantering and enjoying each other's company, her son spent a good portion of the time at the table answering e-mails.

Of course I understand his desire to get tasks done, but it was a Saturday evening and his mother's birthday, and the evening focused on celebrating her. She confided in me that her son's behavior really bothered her and this was her experience with him all the time. I wondered how his team must experience him. How present is he with them? What does he signal with his behavior?

People put all their energy into getting things done but don't stop to think about who they're being in the quest to get those things done. Your intentions may be good, but the impact of your behavior may run counter to those intentions. If people don't feel you are present with them, a part of them stays reserved, not vindictively but in self-preservation. It is an unconscious reaction. When others feel as if they or what they are saying doesn't matter, they will engage differently.

People listen more to what you do than to what you say. Whatever you model will get played out in the organization, so be careful about what you model. If Mary's son starts being more present, it will make a huge difference in how others feel around him. The ripple effect with behavior starts with you.

Who are you being while you are being?

CHAPTER 5

Making a Difference

I hope you have had the good fortune of crossing paths with at least one person during your career who made a difference in your life, your leadership, or how you see yourself. In my career, one of those people was a general manager at one of my first corporate jobs. He ran a global manufacturing company and had a natural ability to act intentionally, helping individuals and businesses thrive. The energy he created in organizations was palpable and translated into dramatic business results. One division he managed went from losing money and at risk of being sold to the most profitable division within a $4 billion dollar company in less than two years. These tangible, real, bottom-line results came from operating with a surprisingly simple recipe, although one whose success is highly dependent on the individual mixing the ingredients. He recognized the impact of his position, actions, and words, and aligned them with purpose. At his core, he knew that his job was to give people something to believe in, through both what he modeled and what he expected. He asserted that when an organization believed in its people and gave them something to believe in, phenomenal things could happen. In three different companies I watched him implement this recipe with success. In each case, he

- *Assessed* the context, both business and organizational (such as market dynamics, customer engagement, product portfolio, organizational culture, and talent).

- *Articulated* a compelling aspiration over and over. This is classic psychological research in action: repetition is a profound method of persuasion. "People have the maximum confidence in an idea after it has been repeated between three and five times."[1]

- *Connected* personally with all employees to share the aspiration and invite their help in achieving it. He made them feel valued, seen, and heard.

Although the steps are clear, their impact rested in the choices he made each day: he chose to be a leader who demonstrated being present, connecting with all the people he came in contact with, believing in them more than they believed in themselves. Who he chose to be made all the difference.

This is the future of leadership: the conscious use of yourself as a leader. It's getting back to an essence of leadership that relies on individual capability, not on the trappings of position.

One person truly can make a difference.

·················· CHAPTER 6 ··················

Using Your Power Intentionally

··

Leadership power comes in two forms: positional and personal. Positional power comes from titles: chief executive officer, vice president, director, or manager. Those with personal power may or may not have titles but their charisma, relationships, and influence draw others to them. When someone has both forms of power, it's a wonderful blend. Regardless of where you fall, understanding how others relate to perceived power is crucial in understanding how to use your own leadership power.

A good friend of mine is a senior executive at a pharmaceutical company. Making the leap to that level in the organization, however, took some adjustment. After one of her first meetings in the new role she called me and said, "I think I blew it."

In her previous role as director, part of her style was thinking out loud; she was a hugely divergent thinker. Her peers welcomed her style; they could share ideas, build on one another's thoughts, and come up with something better than any of them would have alone. As a new vice president in a highly scientific organization, however, her comments landed very differently. In this role, people looked to her for direction. When she offered various ideas on one topic, others experienced her style as indecisive. While her way of operating was well-intentioned, encouraging an approach in which multiple ideas could be considered, others experienced her as not having a clear focus.

We explored how she could continue to create an environment in which people could generate ideas but from a slightly more focused place. We developed a way for her to categorize and prioritize her ideas before voicing them to others: capturing ideas on paper as they came to her, and then consciously choosing how to pace them into the meeting. Once she understood she could operate without constraining her thinking—that it was more about how she presented her many thoughts—both she and the organization benefited.

When she was promoted, people's relationship to her shifted because of her perceived power. She hadn't considered this new context—as the head of her department—and what it meant for how she wanted to come across. As people climb the corporate ladder, these sorts of aha moments are common.

In the same manner, I find many informal leaders do not realize the amount of influence they hold in their organizations; they do not understand how to use their power intentionally. I am currently working on a project with a large cross-functional team. The positional leaders (the senior sponsors) have demonstrated extraordinary attention to the project, working collaboratively, communicating consistently, and ensuring alignment among the stakeholders. However, two informal leaders are not actively engaging with the process. Their personal power in the project shows up in a negative way, particularly as others look to them as a barometer for how fully to engage. These informal leaders are going through the motions and getting the essential work done, but they are withholding their full energy and discretionary effort. While certainly their choice, I don't believe it is a choice they have made consciously or have thought through in terms of the consequences.

- It impacts both the team's morale and performance. While the executive sponsors have laid forth strong inspirational goals, these individuals cause others to question the sincerity of those goals, which diverts energy from critical project work.

- It impacts their personal futures within the organization. Their behavior is being observed by senior leaders and being used to gauge readiness for the next levels of positional leadership.

They shape their destiny simply by who they are being. But it doesn't have to be this way: they can change the future at any time, simply by consciously deciding how they want to show up. So can you.

Use your power wisely.

CHAPTER 7

Matching Impact with Intention

Our intentions don't always show themselves in our actions. I see the impact of this in meetings all the time. At a recent meeting I facilitated, the leader set the stage beautifully. "I really want you to be present over the next two and a half days," she said. "As a global team, we don't get many opportunities to work face to face. Having time to get to know one another and talk about the issues we're facing will have a huge impact on what we can accomplish. I've made an investment in bringing the team together and I hope you'll make an investment by limiting outside distractions and keeping calls and e-mails to a minimum." About ninety minutes into the meeting, she pulled out her laptop and began answering e-mail. When we returned from the first break, attendees followed her lead and pulled out their laptops. She unintentionally had given permission for the exact behavior she said she didn't want present in the meeting. People listen much more to what you do than what you say and this leader spoke volumes with her behavior. What's more, the leader's behavior ran directly counter to what she had said, and when words don't match deeds, trust is undermined. Further, if people learn they can't trust everyday promises, then they start to wonder about bigger commitments, not always in a dramatic way but in more subtle, questioning ways.

Several years ago I worked with a company president who was a functional expert and had all the makings of a great leader, but she scared people. While there was certainly nothing wrong with the high standards she set, she operated in a way that made others fearful of having wrong answers, raising new ideas, and being anything but perfect. Her actions ran completely counter to her intentions: fostering an environment of inclusion, innovation, and excitement about the future. We worked together for about six months and focused on who she was "being," how her actions were being interpreted, and the impact of her actions on the culture of the organization.

For example, she told her team that she valued innovative, out-of-the-box ideas for improving the organization. When they would voice their ideas to her, she would dive into the details of how they could work and look for potential barriers, which was her way of problem solving and thinking through the possibilities. Her team, however, perceived it as wanting a validated business case before bringing ideas forward, that it was not okay to discuss ideas in a more free-flowing, brainstorming fashion. In terms of the organization's performance, this stifled new ideas, innovation, and creative thinking, and resulted in a much more formal atmosphere. It was completely counter to what she wanted to create; her behavior and the team's interpretation of that behavior set a different ball in motion than the one she had intended.

With her consent, I collected some data to help her see the problem more objectively, using direct observation and conversation with selected colleagues. Seeing the data, she was able to focus on how she affected her colleagues and how she could sync her intentions with her desired impact. She prioritized being very intentional in her leadership. Within six months she personally shifted and, in turn, the organization shifted. A renewed energy in the place meant people felt safe to try new ideas, and teams seemed more confident, alive, and connected. The result: multiple innovative ideas made it to the consumer and moved the company forward.

I asked her to reflect on what she believed made the biggest difference in catalyzing the shift and increasing her effectiveness. She said it was when she "got" the concept we had been working on in her coaching: being present in the moment and watching herself in the moment simultaneously. Think about that. It requires enough awareness at any given time to recognize your impact, decide if that impact matches your intention, determine what behaviors may need to change—and how—and then shift those behaviors, all while maintaining the flow of the interaction. It requires substantial brainpower—not to mention practice—but its utility is indisputable. Being present enough that you can flex your behavior to get the result you want is one of the highest forms of self-awareness.

The possibilities of being more intentional are not reserved for individual pursuits; they can be applied to organizational pursuits as well. Three years ago I was at a meeting in a beautiful lodge about ninety minutes outside of Seattle. As the lodge was far from the airport, I had to leave at 4:30 AM to make my flight back to the East Coast. At 4:25 AM on the morning of my departure, I was waiting in the cold and dark for my ride. Four thirty came and went. Four thirty five. Four forty. At 4:45 AM, I called the cab company to ensure that the driver was on his way. The dispatcher promptly checked with the driver and there was no answer. At this point I was getting quite anxious about getting to the airport on time, particularly knowing the long drive ahead. The cab company apologized profusely and dispatched another vehicle to pick me up, noting that this was very unlike the driver and that they were sorry for the inconvenience.

Another cab arrived around 4:55 AM and we were on our way. While I was frustrated, I felt that the company had handled the situation well and chalked it up to the trials of business travel. About two weeks after arriving home from that trip, an envelope came in the mail. It was from the cab company. They sent a card apologizing again and letting me know that the driver had missed our pickup because he had to rush his young daughter to the hospital with a high fever. Thankfully, she came through that fine. They also included a $100 American Express gift certificate for my troubles and wrote, "We pride ourselves on showing up professionally, on time, and with a smile. We failed this time around. Should you ever be out at the Lodge again, we hope we'll get another chance to make it right." Wow—a powerful example of this company being intentional about how it shows up.

One final story to drive the point home. I was in a local Starbucks for my weekend treat of a great cup of coffee. My usual is a decaf triple grande, nonfat, extra-hot latte (now that's a mouthful!). However, on this particular day I was leaning more in the direction of a simple cup of black coffee and told the friend I was with that this was all I was going to have. As I approached the counter, the young barista behind the espresso machine looked at me and said, "Triple grande, nonfat latte?" And while he missed a few details of the order (decaf and extra-hot), I was so impressed that he remembered me from weekend to weekend that I said, "That's right. Wow, that's impressive. Just add decaf and extra hot and we'll be good to go." My friend knows me well and just shook her head and smiled. I asked, "What's the smile about?" She said, "This is your message in action; this isn't just about leadership, this is about life. You had every intention of having a cup of black coffee when you came in here this morning and instead you chose to drink something different in order to reinforce what you thought was great behavior by that barista. All of that went through your head in a split second and you consciously chose in the direction of the barista." She was right.

Now I know that it's an effective sales strategy to know your customers and I know Starbucks trains its employees on creating an inviting, friendly atmosphere. In fact, the opening page of its website says, "It's just a moment in time—just one hand reaching over the counter to present a cup to another outstretched hand. But it's a connection. We make sure everything we do honors that connection." The barista certainly didn't need to act in line with the company philosophy, but as a consumer I'm much more inclined to support a company that makes a personal connection with me and cares about me as a customer than one that does not. So I chose to support not only the barista but the organizational strategy and effort that went behind it. Consumers make the same choice thousands, if not millions, of times a day. It has a very real impact on our organizations and the bottom-line results that are achieved, and it all hinges on individuals and the choices they make. Every moment of every day is an opportunity and a choice.

How have you chosen to behave today?

ROME WAS NOT BUILT IN A DAY
Leading with Intention Takes Practice

In part I, you were asked to look in the mirror and recognize your impact; let's move the concept now from cognitive understanding to behavioral action. Rome was not built in a day and being intentional takes practice; that's what makes the difference between a nice concept you've read about and a fundamental change in how you impact the world. Part II contains tools, ideas, and questions for building your intentionality.

We do not see things as they are,
we see things as we are.

ANONYMOUS

CHAPTER 8

How Do You Practice Leading with Intention? Eight Critical Questions

So, how do you build your capacity to operate more intentionally? The foundation is self-awareness. The rest is practice, consistency, and conscious effort. Below are eight critical questions for beginning to build (or for refreshing) your self-awareness. Before you read further, take some time to reflect on your answers.

1. What kind of environment do you create in your interactions with others?

2. Are you clear about your intentions?

3. Do you have preconceived notions or mind-sets of a person or situation?

4. Do you challenge those mind-sets?

5. How open are you to your own learning?

6. Do you do what you say you are going to do?

7. How would others describe you as a leader?

8. Why do you do the work you do?

---

*A well-placed question
has the power to change an outcome.*

CHAPTER 9

Question #1: What Kind of Environment Do You Create?

As you think about the kind of environment you create, consider the following:

- What kind of environment do you create in your interactions with others? Your behavior in any interaction contributes to the dynamic. How would others describe the dynamic you create?

- Think of the last three meetings you attended. How did you show up? What did you signal with your behavior? What did you contribute? What did you diminish?

- Do you own your contribution in one-on-one meetings, small-group meetings, large groups, and in your family?

- Do you think about how you want to be perceived in your interactions? What would happen if you thought through that more intentionally?

Think of someone in your career who made you better at what you do. Now describe that person and the impact the individual had on your life. If I collected one hundred of those descriptions, there would potentially be one hundred unique ways of influencing others. However, all one hundred of those individuals would have created an environment that was stimulating for at least one other human being. Now think of the impact if each one of us made a decision to intentionally, positively impact the environment of at least one other person. The potential is enormous.

Several years ago I worked with a marketing leader named David. His company had been acquired by a larger one, and he was asked to stay on to launch a product the smaller company was bringing into the newly combined organization. He agreed and began his work of both integrating into the new organization and bringing a new product to market, one that had big expectations from both Wall Street and company executives. Delivering on its potential would require careful orchestration of multiple functional areas (sales, marketing, manufacturing, and distribution), which, by the way, were also geographically dispersed and in the process of merging their people, processes, and cultures.

The culture of the company he entered was fairly conservative, somewhat passive-aggressive, and very hierarchically oriented. David, however, was none of the above. He was more of a maverick: he loved to challenge the status quo and believed that the best answers came from having direct, open conversations with all levels of the organization. He said over and over, "Give people a voice and they will create great outcomes." He lived this phrase in his actions and created forums for people's voices to be heard. His high expectations and tremendous energy were felt in every interaction, be it one-on-one or in front of a large group. He was single-handedly creating a new environment.

In doing this, however, he upset the status quo of the acquiring organization and challenged long-held ways of operating. Although he had roadblocks put in his way by those uncomfortable with his approach, he continued onward. In the end, the product launch was a huge success, the environment was galvanized and energized, and he made each one of the individuals involved in the project better—so much so that those I have followed up with in the years since count it as one of the most significant times in their careers.

Can you say the same of your work? Are you aware of the environment you create? Does it inspire people to be their best?

While David is a great example of how much one person can impact an environment, an environment can also have a significant impact on individuals. Early in my corporate career I was recruited for a job that was outside my comfort zone. As I drove to the first interview, I didn't know why I was considering the position. It was in a new industry for me, one I knew nothing about; I wasn't sure I had the right skills for the job; and

············ GREAT IDEA ·············

Think of the last three meetings you attended. How did you show up? What did you signal with your behavior? What did you contribute? What did you diminish? How could you have operated more intentionally?

to top it off, the offices were an hour and a half from my house. For the entire drive to the first interview, I asked myself, "If I get this job, do I really want to do this every day?"

As soon as I arrived, though, I sensed something about the place—an energy and excitement in the air. People talked about possibilities for the future. They spoke of each other with high regard. Leaders were accessible, knowledgeable, and interested. I noticed an undercurrent of optimism, a belief that, "We can do great things here and we can learn a lot from each other." When I left the interview, I knew I had to find a way to work there. Fortunately, for me, I got that opportunity, and I spent the next several years driving three hours a day just to be part of that environment. It wasn't just me; people from the outside felt it too. And nothing in that feeling had to do directly with the products, the marketing strategies, or the distribution channels of the company; it had to do with the people. To this day I meet people who were in our industry at that time and all of them comment on how remarkable it must have been to be part of that company. Those who worked there remember it as one of the best work experiences of their lives and twenty-plus years later still talk about the company with fondness. Never underestimate the power of environment to impact people in ways that can't even be imagined at the time.

During the next interaction you have, choose consciously, deliberately, and intentionally the environment you want to create. Notice how it feels to operate this way.

Then do it again and again and again; work the muscle until it becomes embedded in the way you operate. I guarantee you will experience more meaningful results.

You are 100 percent responsible
for the tone you set.

CHAPTER 10

Question #2: Are You Clear About Your Intentions?

Perception is reality. Beliefs guide what we perceive, which affects how we act, which determines what we consider possible. When you walk into a meeting, are you clear about your intentions for that meeting? Before you enter have you thought about the dynamics in the room, the key points you want to make, the questions you want to ask, and how you want to show up? Or have you rushed into the room from another meeting with no real sense of what you are walking into or the contribution you want to make? Unfortunately, the second scenario is more common than not and leaves both the outcomes of the meeting and your own performance more to chance than design. You miss the opportunity to lead from a conscious state and intentionally shape the leadership perception of you.

A good tool for building your intentionality is a tool known as the 2+2 (fig. 10.1). I learned this tool from a senior executive who—particularly with his schedule—amazed me with his ability to show up at any meeting seemingly fully prepared and focused on what he wanted to

The 2+2

Two questions I want to ask:

1. _____

_____

2. _____

_____

Two things I want to contribute:

1. _____

_____

2. _____

_____

FIGURE 10.1 Tools for Practice: The 2 + 2

contribute. Before the next meeting you go into this week, do the following: given the dynamics, context, and agenda of the meeting, determine two questions you want to ask and two thoughts you want to contribute. When I introduced this tool to a coaching client, he asked, "Won't being intentional take a lot of time?" Not all interactions and meetings require tons of planning, but all meetings require intention. This tool takes just a moment to use. You can determine your two questions and two contributions as you walk to the meeting. The simple act of being clear in your own mind about your intentions helps you come across as more grounded, prepared, and transparent.

---

*Clarity inspires confidence
and confidence inspires commitment.*

CHAPTER 11

Question #3: Do You Have Preconceived Notions of a Person or a Situation?

Isn't it fascinating that stories from long ago that we hold of ourselves and of others and that others hold of us find their way into our present? And maybe more than just find their way. Some guide our days, invisible in presence but powerful in force. This is a mind-set—a way of looking at the world, a situation, or ourselves; a set of assumptions that guides our actions. Mind-sets can determine whole schools of thought. Mind-sets determine for many of us what we believe is possible.

Mind-sets aren't inherently good or bad, but they are a necessary part of how we function. Without a mind-set to help filter the amount of data coming at us at any given time, we could end up feeling overwhelmed. However, mind-sets also hold great power to help or hinder us in our day-to-day lives. Tacit cognition maps are the filters through which individuals decide what is plausible and possible. Consider what happened when Roger Bannister became the first man to run a sub-four-minute mile on May 6, 1954. Prior to that it was thought impossible to run this distance in less than four minutes. Two months after Bannister's epic accomplishment, two more individuals ran sub-four-minute miles; many attribute that accomplishment to the newfound belief that it could actually be done. In essence, what we *feel* we can influence affects what we actually *do* influence.

New research shows it's more than a Pollyanna outlook or the power of positive thinking, but an idea that has its basis in multiple fields, including neuroscience, quantum physics, and psychology. Science is now proving two important concepts that have long been held as common sense:

- First, "expectation shapes reality."[2] What we expect to happen strongly influences what actually happens. Take, for example, the science behind the placebo effect: in a 2005 study, people given a sugar pill instead of a pain reliever experienced marked and measurable relief comparable to "a clearly analgesic" dose of morphine.[3] Their focus was redirected from their pain to the idea of pain relief, which activated those circuits in the brain. They experienced what they expected.

- Second, "attention density shapes identity."[4] With continued attention, mind-sets become permanent, stable pathways in the brain. This is an idea that began in quantum physics with the Quantum Zeno Effect (QZE), which found that simply observing a system (in this case rapidly decaying beryllium atoms) reduced the rate at which that system changed. UCLA's Jeffrey Schwartz applied the QZE to neuroscience and found that "the mental act of focusing stabilizes the associated brain circuits."[5]

Psychologists and sociologists have put the idea into practice, showing that drawing continued attention to a new idea can cause an increase in positive outcomes. Severely depressed patients focusing regular, ongoing attention on optimism experienced an improvement in their symptoms.[6] Managers given not just training but also follow-up coaching experienced increased productivity.[7]

By paying repeated attention to a new idea or mind-set, it becomes a regular part of our thought processes, which determines how we approach the world and the actions we take as a result. That's a lot of power, knowing that just by changing the way you think about an issue, you can proactively impact the outcomes achieved.

Awareness that each of us has mind-sets from which we operate—and that these mind-sets directly impact our behavior, decisions, and actions—builds one's leadership capacity. Mind-sets are not static; they are dynamic and with new information and/or experience we can shift our mind-sets. The key is being conscious of your mind-sets and open to challenging them.

What are the stories you have of yourself?
Of others?

CHAPTER 12

Question #4: Do You Challenge Your Mind-Sets?

As humans, we pay attention to data that reinforces what we believe. But many leaders do not recognize that they operate from their own worldview. Many believe that what they see is reality, as opposed to their own interpretation of reality. We all have mind-sets; the trick is in understanding the experiences that informed our mind-sets. We are stamped early with filters, triggers, and frames of reference that color how we see the world. The beauty and the power come from being able to stand outside of these and see them, and then consciously choosing how to react rather than simply reacting on instinct. So how do you make your mind-sets visible? You've already taken the first step—you're aware of them. Now that you know they exist, they'll be easier to spot.

One tool that is among the most useful for identifying or deconstructing a mind-set is also one of the simplest. First, look for emotional or physical triggers: any time you feel yourself having a reaction physically or emotionally, take a deep breath and ask yourself the following questions:

- What is happening right now?
- What am I thinking right now about what is happening?
- What am I feeling right now about what is happening?
- What am I doing right now about what is happening?
- What mind-sets and unchallenged conclusions do I carry that might affect how I see this issue?
- What might this issue look like from someone else's point of view?
- What is preventing me from expanding my point of view?
- What am I trying to achieve in this situation?
- What am I doing right now to prevent myself from achieving this end?
- What am I choosing now?

As stated previously, we aren't always conscious of our mind-sets. You must cultivate within yourself the discipline to observe yourself in action, to become aware of what you are doing while you are doing it, how you are being while you are being it, and what you are thinking while you are thinking it. However, just because you recognize a mind-set doesn't necessarily mean you need to change it. It may be perfectly valid. What's important is that you recognize your mind-sets, see their impact on the assumptions you are making and actions you are taking, and then choose your behavior more intentionally.

The difficulty is that since most mind-sets are unconscious and accessed so quickly, they can be difficult to recognize. Our brains move through the cognitive process in a split second: observing data, adding meaning, and choosing an action. When we're thinking so quickly, we often don't realize that our mind-set doesn't fit the situation or that we're acting on incomplete data. As stated previously, we tend to pay attention to data that reinforces what we already believe. This behavior is best illustrated with a tool known as the Ladder of Inference. Developed in 1990 by Chris Argyris, professor emeritus at Harvard Business School until his death in 2013, and popularized by Peter Senge in *The Fifth Discipline*, the Ladder of Inference essentially explains how we make meaning of situations and then operate out of those meanings. It is quite useful in helping us become more aware of our own thinking, making one's thinking and reasoning more visible to others, and inquiring into others' thinking and reasoning. While Argyris had seven rungs on his ladder, I've streamlined it to four: the observable event, the filters that emerge, the assumptions we make, and the actions we take (fig. 12.1).

Let's look at how this plays out in real life. The brain is designed to help us quickly filter through mounds of stimuli; if we don't have all the information about a given situation, we fill in the blanks. We create a story. Recently, I sent an e-mail to a client to ask a question about a project we worked on in the past. We have always enjoyed a great partnership and have done a few projects together. One week passed and I hadn't heard anything back; as he usually responds quickly to e-mail I was a little surprised but figured he might be traveling or on vacation and simply had not put an out-of-office message on his e-mail. After two weeks passed I e-mailed

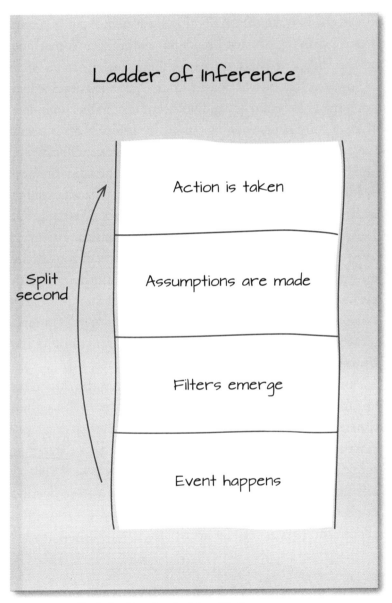

FIGURE 12.1 Tools for Practice: Ladder of Inference

once again, thinking that my message may have just been lost in the barrage of e-mails that most people get in a day. When I didn't hear back I made up a story that something odd had happened between us, although I was not sure what or how, and that he was upset with me. I decided that I would not e-mail him again as I did not want him to feel hounded. Then one Thursday evening, about three weeks after I sent the original e-mail, a note popped up in to my mailbox from him. He explained that he had been out of the office on family leave; he had been overwhelmed with what he was dealing with on that front and had simply lost track of e-mails. Of course I let him know that I completely understood, but it caused me to pause and think about where I had gone in my interpretation. I had filled in the void of information with my own interpretation and acted out of that story. As Larry Wilson and Hersch Wilson wrote in *Play to Win*, "No matter where we went to school, we're all graduates of MSU, the University of Making Stuff Up."[8]

This cycle happens thousands of times a day. The trick lies in learning to recognize your mind-sets and deciding consciously what you then want to do, rather than simply reacting out of an unexamined mind-set with a pattern of thinking that may or may not be serving you well. Today's business environment requires the ability to see beyond one's own perspective. What stories are you making up about others? What stories are others making up about you?

Shape your mind-sets or your mind-sets will shape you.

CHAPTER 13

Question #5: How Open Are You to Your Own Learning?

In my work with executives I find that those who have the most profound impact on organizations are those who are open to their own learning, operate with a degree of humility, and encourage diverse viewpoints. They are not afraid to be a bit vulnerable and not have all the answers; they know that vulnerability connects people and makes them more human. At some level, we all crave this humanity, this sense of connection and are drawn to leaders who model this way of being.

Late in my corporate career, I led an effort to establish a "culture of development" across five distinct business units spanning North and South America. When I started that job, my boss gave me a clear directive not to be in my office more than 50 percent of the time. He believed that without my getting out and talking to others in the company and experiencing the different locations firsthand, the initiative had little chance for success. He knew that an effort such as this would require an environment in which I was actively engaging the organization, testing my ideas with others, and incorporating their feedback. He was right: creating the space for others to offer feedback, opinions, and ideas generated tremendous momentum for the work.

One tool that I used to do this was a mind map (fig. 13.1). A mind map is essentially a visual representation of brainstorming. It is a nonlinear way of organizing information that allows you to capture the natural flow of ideas. It begins with a central idea or image placed in a circle in the middle of a page. As more ideas emerge, they are captured as lines branching from the central idea. As ideas expand, more branches and subbranches are added. An important tenet of this tool is to put down all ideas without judgment or evaluation. Sometimes you see relationships and connections immediately, sometimes you don't. Organization of the ideas can always come later; the first requirement is to get the ideas out of your head and onto paper.

Given that I was tasked with establishing a culture of development, I placed a four-by-six-foot sheet of banner paper outside my office and asked the organization to help me build a mind map around this idea. I provided a few starter ideas and left pens near the paper for others to add their ideas as they passed by. Within one week of my posting the mind map outside my office, almost the entire paper had been filled, providing me with a rich base of data from which to build a road map for establishing a culture of development.

People will nurture what they help create. I learned that the sheer act of being open to input and my own learning created better business results and a faster uptake on the goals we had for this project. The approach unlocked

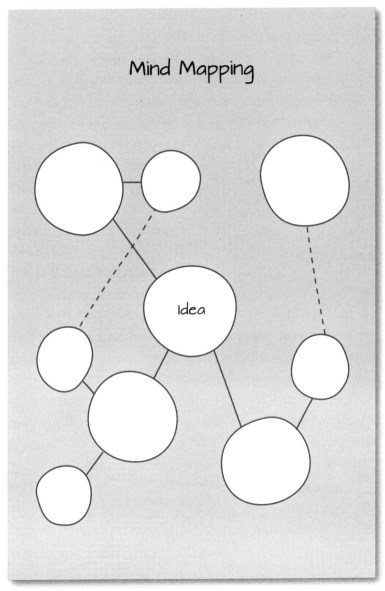

FIGURE 13.1 Mind Mapping (Concept popularized by Tony Buzan, www.thinkbuzan.com)

hidden capacity in the organization and created a new way of thinking about projects of this scale.

So what does it look like to be open to your own learning? It shows up as being curious, open to new ideas, and receptive to different points of view. One way to strengthen this ability is to challenge yourself to do something new every year. At the end of each year, identify two experiences you have never had and commit to making those happen in the coming year. They don't necessarily need to be work-related. For me one year it was riding a Greyhound bus and having high tea at the Four Seasons—two new experiences that exposed me to different people, environments, and learning, and that opened my mind to new perspectives. As you think about yourself, how open are you to your own learning, to changing what isn't working, to seeking out new experiences, and to not being defensive of diverse opinions even when they are radically different than your own? What is one new experience that you will explore this year?

········· GREAT IDEA ·········

At the end of each year, identify two experiences you have never had and commit to making them happen in the coming year.

Try something new.

CHAPTER 14

Question #6: Do You Do What You Say You Are Going to Do?

One of the fastest ways to build trust in any relationship is to do what you say you are going to do. Given that trust is a foundational element in high-performing teams and organizations, be sure to consider your own performance against the metric of following through on commitments. Remember, people pay more attention to what you do than what you say, and your behavior speaks volumes. Case in point: I am working with a company right now whose leaders say that the project we are working on is priority number one for the success of a key division in the company. In fact, they have communicated this to the organization to illustrate the importance they are attaching to the work and to make sure others prioritize requests related to this work. However, in the last two months, four key meetings have been postponed and in two other meetings the main sponsors have not shown up. So what do you think this says to the people in the organization? How do you think others will choose to engage? What do you believe they will think about the leaders who said one thing and are doing another? When credibility gets undermined people stop believing and the success of the effort gets compromised. Bottom-line impact often teeters on choices that seem inconsequential but have tremendous impact. Do you do what you say you are going to do?

Actions speak louder than words.

CHAPTER 15

Question #7: How Would Others Describe You as a Leader?

In our Western practice of organizational life, we are consumers of the "just give me the CliffsNotes, the ten steps, the McManagement answer to solve a problem" approach. So while we may have gained speed in looking for the shorthand solution, I wonder if we haven't lost a critical element of success—the ability to truly connect and inspire. When I watch the most talented leaders with whom I've had the pleasure of working, I notice how people gravitate toward them. People want to get to know them better. They listen. They are okay not having all the answers. They use their single most powerful tool to make a difference in the lives of those they lead: they use themselves. As a leader, how would people describe you? Do they experience you as present, genuine, trustworthy, and inspiring? Do they feel a sense of connection with you?

Recently I was invited to attend a meeting at a Fortune 50 company. Sitting around the table were ten senior executives; the topic under discussion was an acquisition.

A weighty topic for sure and one made more complex by the proposed structure of the deal. I found myself, as I often do, observing the dynamics in the room and the behavior of those around the table. What astonished me was that at literally no point during the two-hour meeting was there a time when one—or more—of the executives were not on their computer or smartphone. At one point in the meeting a vice president of finance, who reported to one of the executives at the table, came in to present some of the financial considerations for the acquisition. Even this topic did not change the behavior in the room. I wondered what the vice president's perception was as she left the room, if she perceived the executive team as disrespectful or disinterested or a thousand other stories that could arise from their behavior. I wondered if the executives realized they were setting a story in motion about this acquisition, at least in her mind. I wondered what stories she would carry back to the organization, whether through her words or actions, about the importance of this acquisition and how much of their energy people should invest in it. And finally, I wondered what the executive team would have done differently if they were being intentional in their leadership.

In this world of hyperconnectivity and 24/7 business hours, have we lost the ability to be in the moment with someone, to not look past the person to the next e-mail coming in, to be present in our leadership and therefore more capable of achieving extraordinary results? Since the feeling of connection is shaped through a series of individual interactions, interactions are a leader's currency.

Extrapolating that premise to a practical application, leaders must actively manage their presence in every inter- action, both formal and informal.

How would you like others to describe you?
What do you do to embody that?

CHAPTER 16

Question #8: Why Do You Do the Work You Do?

Think about the days of the John F. Kennedy administration and the bold aspiration of putting a man on the moon, or Rosa Parks's courage, strength, and clarity of conviction that started this country on a path of change from which it would never be the same. Those were transformative times of great purpose, great courage, and great connection to something larger than ourselves. We are again living on the edge of transformative times in need of great courage, conviction, and connection. In fact, the need for leaders who can truly connect may have never been greater. Transacting commerce is small time; transforming the way business gets done is the big leagues. The world needs big-league players.

> GREAT IDEA
>
> *Identify the words you want to live by. Try to use as few words as possible (certainly no more than seven to ten). Ask yourself, "How does this philosophy show up in my actions? Is there more I can do to bring these words to life?"*

So why do you do the work you do? What is your purpose? What are the words you live by and want to be known by? In my work, I have eight simple words that describe why I do the work I do: "I want it to matter that we met." The shape of those words in my professional life can be as large scale as a total organizational initiative or as individual as executive coaching. No matter what shape it takes, the core remains the same—I want it to matter that we met. So why do you do the work you do? What are your words? Ask yourself these questions:

- In what areas of my professional life would I like to have a greater impact?

- What is preventing me from having that impact?

- When was the last time I felt like I couldn't make a difference? What could I have done to change that feeling?

- What would I do differently if I thought anything was possible?

Reflecting, seeking objective input, and acting with intention—none of these entail an investment of anything more than discipline and time. However, I guarantee that the return on that investment will be significant for a lifetime.

---

*If you didn't have to worry about money,
what would you do at this point in your career?
In your life?*

PART III

A COMMUNICATIONS DEPARTMENT OF ONE

Being Intentional in Your Communication

In my experience, communications is one of the most overlooked and poorly executed areas in many organizations because leaders tend to see it as the responsibility of the communications department rather than owning it as a core component of their leadership.

Where part II focused on your behavior, this section focuses on your communications. Determining how best to communicate in any given situation is both a skill and an art. It requires the same deliberate focus and attention that building your self-awareness does. So while content is important, never underestimate the impact of how a message is delivered. Let's look at how to be more intentional in your communications by being aware of your verbal and nonverbal impact, managing the story of you, customizing your communications, staying in conversations, and being courageous.

Motivating people over time requires, first,
that vision and strategies be communicated on a
continual basis, not just once or occasionally.
That communication must go beyond just informing;
it must excite people by connecting to their values.

JOHN KOTTER

CHAPTER 17

Becoming Aware of Your Verbal and Nonverbal Impact

While we spend a lot of time learning to speak and an even greater amount of time perfecting this ability, we typically do not spend a similar amount of time learning how to listen. The idea of listening as a skill is an unfamiliar notion. As adults, when we think about communication skills, we typically think about speaking and language. However, if you look at how we assess the development of communication across the first few years of an infant's life, the definition is much broader. Pediatricians ask questions like

- Does the infant smile when she sees someone's face?
- Does she follow sounds with her eyes?
- Does she respond to changes in tone of voice?
- Does she laugh?
- Does she communicate using gestures?

Pediatricians look for signs that infants are able to both respond to stimuli and express themselves. As adults, then, why do we rarely consider listening and nonverbal skills as communication skills to actively develop?

If you've ever used American Sign Language (ASL), you know that it's not enough to simply make the signs. A significant portion of the meaning is carried through the facial expression and emotion with which the sign is delivered. When done well, it involves the whole body. In ASL, visual feedback is also paramount; in fact, it's impossible to have a conversation unless you can see that the other person is paying attention. Likewise, your "presence" in interactions is continually transmitted by a series of verbal and nonverbal cues (fig 17.1). What verbal and nonverbal cues are you sending that indicate you are actively listening?

When you commit to being fully present, you send a message that others in the conversation are important to you, that their opinions and time are valuable. By choosing to actively listen rather than passively hear, you forge positive connections that enhance your leadership impact and ultimately the company's bottom line. Active listening creates new possibilities and directly impacts the outcomes achieved, and it all begins with simply making a choice to interact with people more fully, realizing that communicating is about more than talking. When people feel heard, they feel valued.

We learn from birth that when body language and verbal language don't match, the body language is speaking the truth. In fact, experts in the field of communication often quote the "55/38/7 rule," which states that people derive only about 7 percent of the meaning of a communication from the words the speaker uses (verbalized emotion),

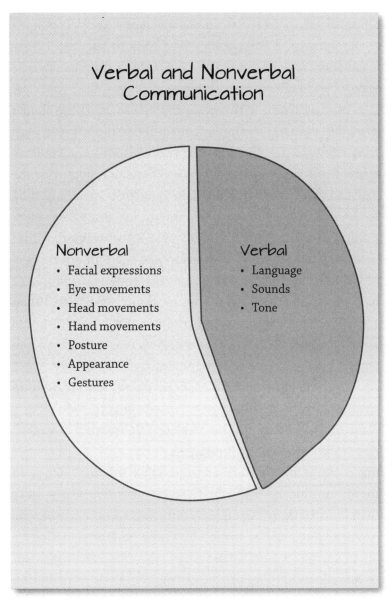

FIGURE 17.1 Verbal and Nonverbal Communication

about 38 percent from the speaker's tone of voice, and a whopping 55 percent from the speaker's body language.[9] Although tested and documented back in the late 1960s, it is widely accepted that the same rule of thumb is true in today's ways of communicating.

An interaction with one of my recent coaching clients provides a perfect example. This individual struggled with how she was perceived in the organization: she couldn't understand why others didn't see the same potential she saw in herself and felt that their perceptions were getting in the way of her ability to get things done. Since a key component of my coaching model is real-life observation, I sat in on several meetings and also viewed a video recording of a presentation that she gave. It was important for me to gain firsthand knowledge of her on-the-job behavior. When I had the opportunity to both observe her in action and watch her in a more formal setting such as a presentation, the gaps in perceived ability became quite clear.

Her perception of the way she operated and the way she actually operated were not congruent. Her verbal and nonverbal language, in the meetings I observed, distanced her from the audience. First, her choice of language did not meet her audiences "where they were living"; she used highly conceptual language for audiences that wanted the nuts and bolts of an implementation plan. Second, she physically positioned herself behind a podium, creating an air of formality and separateness that did not lend itself to a feeling that "we are all in this together." Finally, she did not pay attention to the nonverbal cues she was getting from the various groups I observed. For example, many people were staring off into space or texting. Had she paid attention to these nonverbal messages, she could have adjusted her presentation, asked a thought-provoking question, or physically shifted her location from behind the podium to create more of a connection with her audiences. As we reviewed the notes from the meetings and watched the videotape from her presentation, the gap between intention and impact became clear to her. It was a moment of epiphany. Within the week, we built an action plan to significantly improve both her verbal and nonverbal skills. When I shadowed her at a meeting a month later, I could not believe the difference in impact that she had in the room: she was engaging, connected to the audience, and highly effective—a testament to the fact that these skills are teachable and easily improved with discipline and commitment.

Be present—verbally and nonverbally.
Pay attention to how you are listening.

CHAPTER 18

Managing the Story of You

Whether shaped by mind-sets, experience, or lack of information, we all create stories day in and day out trying to make sense of our world. Given very little information, we quickly make up our own narratives about a situation or a person and then operate through the lens of those stories. When the story of you is something you can adjust, it is kind of ridiculous to leave it to chance, but I cannot tell you how many leaders do just that. I hear time and again, "I'll just let my hard work speak for itself." While a nice sentiment, the reality is that hard work often doesn't speak for itself (or at least it doesn't tell the whole story); *you* have to speak for your hard work. Hard work can never stand alone as the indicator of your ability; to think otherwise is naive and self-defeating. You must actively shape the perception others have of you and your abilities, not in a self-aggrandizing way but in a way that does not leave the story of you to be shaped by others. I believe that people sometimes struggle with the concept of managing their story because they perceive it as playing corporate politics.

Shaping the narrative of you is not political unless that is your intention; shaping your narrative is simply smart.

Six months ago I was working with a client who was a go-getter with equal doses of humility, self-awareness, and ambition. He had built a successful sales and marketing career in typical fashion, toggling between jobs in sales and marketing with increasing scopes of responsibility. He achieved great success at a young age, had a wife with a professional career, had three lovely children, and was the picture of the all-American corporate success story. What people didn't know about him was that he had a deep desire to work in Asia and challenge himself outside of the United States. He believed that when people saw the merit of his accomplishments, they would seek him out for other exciting opportunities. This was true in one sense in that he had received plenty of opportunities over the years, but all were based in the United States.

After several weeks of encouraging him to talk with his boss and explore the possibilities of an assignment in Asia, he finally did so. The response: his boss was stunned and disappointed. Why? The boss had assumed that with the way his career was going and with his family situation (a working spouse, kids in good schools), he would not be open to a change. He had just placed another individual with a similar background in Singapore for a three-year assignment. An opportunity was lost because of a story. It wasn't created from an ill-intentioned place, simply from the facts as the boss perceived them. What's telling about this example is that it is the stories we get locked behind,

The Rule of Three

Manage the story of you.

Three messages you want out there about yourself:

1. _____
   _____

2. _____
   _____

3. _____
   _____

Three people you want to know those messages:

1. _____
   _____

2. _____
   _____

3. _____
   _____

Three actions you will take to make this possible:

1. _____

2. _____

3. _____

FIGURE 18.1 Tools for Practice: The Rule of Three

not the facts. Stories matter and they are within your power to manage. Don't leave it to chance or assumption.

A good tool for managing the story of you is the Rule of Three (fig. 18.1). First, determine three messages about yourself you'd like others to know. Second, identify three people you want to hear those messages. Third, choose three actions you will take to make this possible.

The tool's power lies in its simplicity. Keep your messages and your actions short and crisp. The result is a clear, easily remembered plan for guiding your day-to-day interactions. While there is certainly a place for more complex message maps, my experience with tools is that the easier they are to retain, the more readily you will use them.

Good work doesn't speak for itself;
you must speak for your good work.

CHAPTER 19

Customizing Your Communication

Two points are important to consider when customizing your communications: the language you use and the approach you take.

With regard to the language you use, you have to engage people emotionally more than intellectually to move an organization. Business rhetoric and jargon create barriers to understanding and effectiveness. As language allows immediate access to the cognitive parts of our brains, it is both smart and important to be mindful of it. Your ability to speak in language that can be heard and understood, which does not separate but rather draws people in, is critical for the personal impact you hope to have.

With regard to your approach, people will engage with you on most any idea based primarily on two dimensions: their level of agreement with the idea and their level of personal trust either in you or in your ability to bring the idea to life. Understanding how to orient your communication based on these dimensions is a useful way to think about customizing your approach. The Agreement-Trust Matrix (fig. 19.1) is a great stakeholder management tool that will help you communicate more intentionally. This tool is based on the premise that people respond best when you are willing to meet them where they live. Answer their questions and concerns first and you'll be more likely to have a productive outcome.

The tool is best used to help you form your approach when planning an initiative. In just three steps, you'll create a powerful picture of the dynamics around your efforts:

- Step 1—Make a short list of the people you need to communicate with who are involved in or impacted by your initiative.

- Step 2—Use the matrix to plot the individuals according to the following dimensions:

  - Their agreement with your initiative.

  - Their level of trust in you personally or in your ability to successfully implement the initiative.

- Step 3—Based on this diagram, decide which strategies and approaches are best for how you want to communicate with those who fall in each of the quadrants:

  - Allies are among your best resources. Leverage these relationships to help you raise the agreement and/ or trust of those in other quadrants.

  - Buds can be great sounding boards. Ask those who fall in this quadrant why they have less agreement with the initiative. Given their high trust in you, you are more likely to get honest feedback. Use that data to help improve your approach or craft communications that address the questions or concerns they have raised.

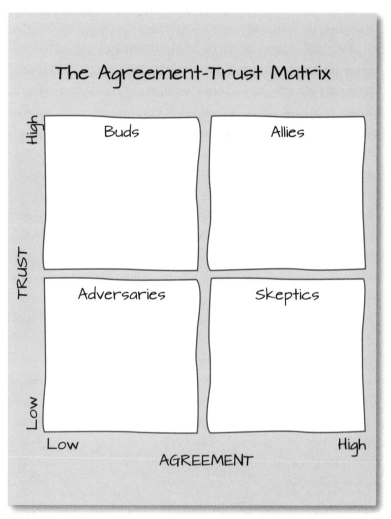

FIGURE 19.1 Tools for Practice: The Agreement-Trust Matrix

- Skeptics have high agreement with the idea but less trust in you or in your ability to pull it off. This could be based on past experience or simply from a lack of exposure to you. In either case, involve them in shaping the idea and providing input on its implementation. This will afford them the opportunity to work more closely with you and develop a higher level of trust in you personally or in your abilities.

- Since adversaries have low agreement and trust, it is best to leverage your allies or even your buds to help move the idea forward. Trying to do that alone is hardly ever an effective strategy; this is an instance where putting a meeting together with you, a skeptic, and an ally or bud would be very beneficial. If you believe a skeptic may try to actively derail the initiative, develop good contingency plans for undesirable but possible actions the skeptic might take.

- If the majority of individuals fall in the lower agreement and trust quadrants (especially in the adversaries quadrant), consider if now is the best time to implement your idea; you may have greater success implementing the idea if you begin at another time.

Case in point: A few years ago I was coaching an individual who had been tasked by her CEO with implementing an executive development initiative in the organization. She was getting very little traction for the initiative and felt both frustrated and unsuccessful in her abilities. She was concerned that her inability to get this initiative off the ground would have an impact on her standing with the CEO. She was right: he was starting to question whether she was the right person for the job. We used the Agreement-Trust Matrix to plot her perceptions of where the top ten key stakeholders of this initiative fell within the quadrants. The resulting picture was a bit overwhelming: all of the key stakeholders fell either in the adversaries or skeptics quadrants! When she saw the picture in its totality, she was stunned. Her first reaction was to feel defeated but after some conversation I encouraged her to see the result more as an opening. She could recommend that the organization was simply not ready for this kind of work at this time and instead provide the CEO with an action plan for advancing the organization's readiness. She did just that and the CEO was delighted. They decided to take a step back and not invest in executive development in that particular year. Instead they created initiatives that focused the stakeholders on the value of executive development and subsequently launched a very successful executive development initiative the following year.

This tool, along with the others in the book, is built to help you be more intentional in everything you do. You will find that the more often you use these tools, the more quickly they will simply become part of the way you think and operate.

Meet people where they live.

CHAPTER 20

Staying in the Conversation

Truth telling became a critical part of the post-apartheid healing process for South Africa and its people. After the first democratic election in 1994, in which all were equally given the right to vote, the newly elected president, Nelson Mandela, faced the problem of how to deal with mass racial oppression and violations of human rights that had occurred during apartheid. (Mandela himself was jailed for twenty-seven years for political activism against apartheid.) Within the country there were many opinions on how the reconciliation process should take place but, ultimately, under the guidance of President Mandela and Archbishop Desmond Tutu, the Truth and Reconciliation Commission (TRC) was formed to provide the opportunity for both victims and oppressors to share their stories from years of apartheid. Victims of gross human-rights violations were encouraged to talk about the impact of such violations in their lives; perpetrators were provided with the opportunity to give testimony on the impact of provoking such abuses. The result was significant healing in the country.

What, might you ask, does this have to do with leading with intention? Everything—it personifies the power of staying in conversation with one another even when it is hard. Far too often when we get frustrated or bored, we opt out—emotionally or even physically—from conversations that we deem difficult or uninteresting, particularly if there is a point of tension. These are the moments when it is crucial that you stay in the conversation and choose in the direction of what you can learn from the interaction, and intentionally manage how you are showing up. Outcomes are created in your world as a result of conversations either with yourself or with others. Think of the last time you left a conversation—emotionally or physically. What were the circumstances? What do you need to do to be capable of staying in difficult conversations? If you are willing to stay in a conversation long enough to truly hear another, you can achieve anything.

---

*How willing are you to stay engaged
in difficult conversations?*

CHAPTER 21

Being Courageous

Mark Twain said, "Courage is resistance to fear, mastery of fear—not absence of fear." If you are going to be an individual who leads with intention, there will inevitably be at least two distinct situations in which your courage will be tested and a conscious choice of who you want to be will come into focus:

- When you have to step out on the "skinny branch" and say something that may be controversial. The skinny branch is a metaphor for the fragility and precariousness of such a situation, like stepping out on the skinny branch of a tree when you're not quite sure if it will bend or break.

- When you have to sense and say what is "hanging in the air"; essentially, when you read the dynamics in a room and must decide whether or not to share with candor what you observe.

Both require courage, care, and tact. Think back on meetings you've been in when thoughts hanging in the air were left unsaid. Why did you choose not to speak up? What was the impact of that choice? How would the situation have been different if people had been willing to address the elephant in the room? What could have been achieved? So much of what needs to be said gets swallowed and so much potential gets left on the table when we prevent ourselves from stepping out on the skinny branch. Ironically enough, courage is built through fear; growth comes in moving through those experiences that make you afraid.

The game changer here is how: the timing of when you speak up, the language you use, and the tone you choose. How you step into those moments when your courage is needed is a critical time of intentionality. It requires an appreciation that finesse is as important as moxie and that maintaining the dignity of all involved is a guiding principle that will serve you well.

The trick, of course, is to master the ability to make these decisions in the moment, to recognize what is hanging in the air, decide whether more is to be gained or lost by speaking up, and then consciously choose how to act—all while maintaining the flow of a conversation. It is possible—it just takes practice.

Never being afraid is unrealistic;
learning to be brave is invaluable.

PART IV

NO ONE WORKS ALONE
Impacting Your Organization

It is time to expand our scope. While the first three parts of this book focus primarily on you and building your self-awareness, parts IV and V consider the larger context in which you operate and how you can best impact your organization and the world.

In part IV, we'll begin by understanding your organizational context and how it should inform your approach. We'll discuss organizational—as opposed to functional—leadership, your role in shaping culture, and the specific challenges of starting a new job, leading a team, and working globally.

No one works alone in an organization, and a world of opportunity awaits those who can work effectively with others.

It is context that gives events meaning.

ANONYMOUS

CHAPTER 22

Knowing the Context

No one lives in a vacuum; we impact and are impacted by both our environment and one another. So while the "use of self" forms the foundation in leading with intention, it is not enough. We all operate—whether willingly or begrudgingly—within a context, be it cultural, organizational, or familial. Context is the air around us; it encompasses the set of circumstances, conditions, and events that surrounds an interaction. Often subtler and more nuanced than explicit, it is a key element to consider in how you choose to show up. Context is intermingled with every interaction we have. The interpersonal or organizational context you work in has likely shaped much of your mind-set and the mind-sets of your colleagues. If you're going into a meeting with a coworker with whom you have a long history and a strong friendship, you will most likely operate differently than if going into a meeting with someone you've met only once under unpleasant circumstances. The same holds true on an organizational level. Your effectiveness increases when you take into consideration elements like recent performance, morale, and major events like mergers or restructurings.

This context will help you determine not only *what* to do but also *how* to do it. If you are operating in an organization where "having the facts" is revered, you will have greater success if you operate from a place of supporting your ideas with data. Context impacts your approach either consciously or subconsciously. It operates as an "if-then" proposition: if your currency is in your interactions, then understanding the context of those interactions (how you are perceived, what the environment is like, where you are starting from) increases your capacity to consciously shape the outcome.

A great tool to help identify the context in which you are working and achieve stronger outcomes is the Context T-Chart (fig. 22.1). It helps identify both the context in which you operate and the best way to "enter" that context to achieve optimal results. On the left-hand side, describe the culture of the organization in which you are working (i.e., project team, department, company); use words that paint the picture of the environment. On the right-hand side, describe how others see you; be as honest with yourself as you can. What do you believe is the perception of you by the organization on which you are focusing this diagnostic? This tool is designed to determine the best way for you to engage with a system: your best entry point. From there, you decide what you need to do to customize your approach and realize your best outcome. This level of intention and deliberateness yields greater results and is all about operating from a place of choice, not circumstance.

As I mentally prepare on my way to each meeting, I consider the context I'll be walking into. Of course it is

FIGURE 22.1 Tools for Practice: Context T-Chart

important to remember that these are my perceptions alone, so it is good to test those perceptions. Sometimes I do that overtly, sometimes less so. Sometimes I'll reach out to a trusted colleague or two and say, "Here's my read on this. Does that sound right?" More often, though, it's subtler. I'll test my perceptions by asking questions during the meeting or simply by being hyperattuned to the conversation; some of the best data I get is by observing body language and hearing the tone of voice used.

A coaching client with whom I worked experienced this firsthand when he moved across the country with the same company. While he assumed that much of the context in which he would be working would be the same, it was, in fact, quite different. The context of the New York office was one of fast-paced banter and quick decisions; the context of the Portland office was deeper deliberations and a more considered approach to decision making. He struggled for the first couple of months and created the story that the Portland office was not as high performing as the New York office, which was absolutely not the case in terms of financial outcomes and customer results. When we began working together, we took a step back to consider the context in which he was working and the image of him and developed strategies for a better entry point for him in the Portland office. He adjusted his approach by asking more questions that could be deliberated among the group versus simply looking for validation of his point of view. This created more connection between him and the team and a wider perspective from which to determine his next actions. Within two months he was feeling better about the move, performing at a higher level, and contributing to the Portland office in a much more productive way. Context reading is a fundamental skill of an effective organizational leader.

What is your entry point?

CHAPTER 23

Moving Beyond Functional Expertise

Many leaders have risen through the ranks based primarily on how they've performed in a particular function, whether that's as a salesperson who can close the deal, a manufacturer who can increase output, or a scientist who can discover new scientific insights. They've essentially been rewarded for the behavior of being functionally excellent. The irony in this is that as individuals climb higher in organizations, functional skills are not a differentiator of great leadership or a source of long-term competitive advantage; they are merely the "price of entry," the baseline expectation. Think of your leadership on a bigger stage; don't confine it to the functional area you now lead—what other venues need your passion, capability, and energy? In this day and age, being a successful leader requires much more than just functional expertise: it requires leaders who can make connections across the company; who understand how to use their functional expertise in support of larger organizational initiatives; and who can mobilize human energy, shape culture, and lead change. Businesses need leaders who can create environments that attract talented, engaged employees, and then inspire them. Rather than functional leaders, they need organizational leaders who operate from a centered understanding of themselves and their environment.

And while systematic processes for developing functional skills are carried out daily at business schools worldwide, much less attention is given to the development of skills for organizational leadership. Frequently the necessary skills— leading with intention, building engagement, and shaping culture—are dismissed as soft, implying a judgment on both their value and the ease of their acquisition. Leaders can no longer afford to let their development in these areas happen by chance; building these skills takes commitment.

Too often executives allow what they do in their functional roles to define who they are as leaders. I suggest that a much more productive model is to flip that: to first identify who you want to be as a leader and then let that knowledge guide the deliberate choice of leadership actions—to guide what you do. I call it the "Being and Doing" model (fig. 23.1).

Stay focused on who you are being while you are doing and a deep awareness will emerge from the simple act of paying attention to this flip. In fact, medical research supports the notion that when we make a conscious choice to do something, it changes the way the brain functions; that when we commit to a new possibility, it alters who we are and transforms how we behave.[10] Remember, no one works alone in an organization; who you are being has a direct impact on how the organization operates and the results that can be achieved.

Who are you being while you are doing?

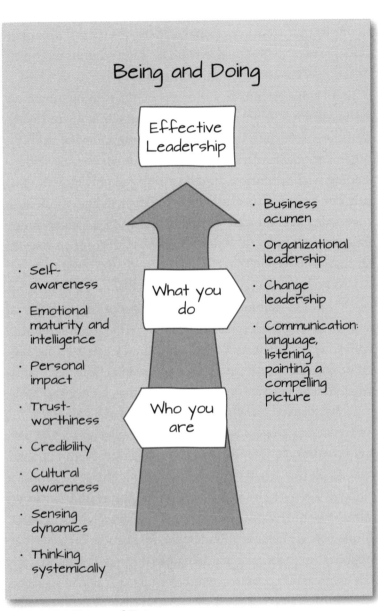

Being and Doing

Effective Leadership

- Self-awareness
- Emotional maturity and intelligence
- Personal impact
- Trust-worthiness
- Credibility
- Cultural awareness
- Sensing dynamics
- Thinking systemically

What you do

Who you are

- Business acumen
- Organizational leadership
- Change leadership
- Communication: language, listening, painting a compelling picture

FIGURE 23.1 Being and Doing

CHAPTER 24

Sending a Man to the Moon

We witness examples of the impact of who one is being throughout history. Take for example the year 1961: John F. Kennedy laid forth a bold goal to land a man on the moon and return him safely to Earth. He by no means accomplished that herculean task on his own. While he set the vision, thousands of others brought that vision to life. What motivated them to do so? Kennedy himself motivated others through both what he represented and how he was perceived as a leader. In fact, one famous story is about President Kennedy touring NASA facilities late in 1961 and greeting employees. As he shook one gentleman's hand, he asked, "What is your job here at NASA?" The man replied, "I'm sending a man to the moon." The man was a janitor.

One person can set the tone for an entire country, bring a vision to life, and set a ball in motion for an organization, a country, and the world. John F. Kennedy made the declaration of "putting a man on the moon by the end of the decade" and the country responded; he painted the picture of what was possible and turned that picture into a reality.

And just as he did not work alone to accomplish this, neither do you work alone in your organization.

I'll share one additional story, as we often don't believe in the power we each have to move an organization. This is a story about Ms. Roslyn, a security-line agent at the Philadelphia International Airport.

It was the Sunday after Thanksgiving, around 1:00 PM. I was on my way to a business meeting in Toronto that began the next morning. It was a cold, damp day in Philadelphia and I was standing with a long line of people waiting to go through airport security. As it was the end of a holiday weekend, fairly dreary outside, and a slow-moving line, the mood, as you can imagine, was not pleasant. As I waited in line for my turn at the security podium, a line agent announced to the long line of people who she was and what she was doing there. It went something like this: "Well, hello travelers! My name is Ms. Roslyn and I'm very glad to have you here today. I like knowing that I play a part in getting you where you want to go, but I'm looking out here at your faces and they are not looking all that happy. C'mon people, you've just had a holiday break, you've been with loved ones, let's see some smiles out there." The response was lukewarm at best: some cracked half-smiles, and some just tried to make her feel better by acknowledging her presence. By and large, people were surprised but not terribly moved by her comments.

Then she did something that changed the entire culture of that security line: she noticed a serviceman and his wife at the back of the line and she said, "Young man, are you serving our country?" She said it loud enough for all of us to hear. He replied, "Yes ma'am, I am." She asked, "Active duty?" He replied, "Yes ma'am, active duty just home for a short leave." She then said, "Well, young man, you and your wife come with me." She proceeded to escort them to the front of the line and said to all of us standing there. "People, let's show this couple some love. They are serving our country; they are making sacrifices for all of us; they deserve to be thanked." And then what happened was unbelievable for an airport security line—spontaneous applause broke out and people shook the young couple's hands and patted them on the back as they walked to the front of the line.

No one grumbled about them cutting in line, smiles appeared on faces, and for that moment we were all joined in a culture of appreciation for this young serviceman and his wife; and although they were somewhat embarrassed by the attention, a key point about culture came through in vivid color: that the most potent way culture gets shaped is by what a leader models. And in that space and for that time, Ms. Roslyn was the leader of that security line, shaping its culture. We can all certainly learn from Ms. Roslyn; she chose how she was going to show up, she made a conscious choice to change the tenor of that security line, and she acted.

How do you impact the culture and tone of the organization?
How does the culture and tone impact you?

CHAPTER 25

Shaping a Culture
or Letting a Culture Shape You

Culture will develop by design or default; an organization's ability to shape its culture is determined primarily by its level of intention. I am passionate about culture because of its power to unlock potential or shut it down; to facilitate extraordinary outcomes or incremental ones; to infuse energy or drain it. Culture is often experienced as amorphous in concept but critical to organizational success. A case in point: In 1986 the United States space program witnessed an awful tragedy when the space shuttle *Challenger* exploded as it climbed through the atmosphere. Seven astronauts, including America's first teacher in space, Christa McAuliffe, lost their lives that fateful morning. At that time, investigations pointed to NASA's organizational culture as a key contributor to the disaster.

Fast forward to 2003, seventeen years later, and the space shuttle *Columbia* experienced a similar tragedy just moments before it was scheduled to land after a successful sixteen-day mission. Again, seven brave astronauts lost their lives. The Columbia Accident Investigation Board report identified NASA's culture as one of the chief contributors to the Columbia disaster. The report pointed to ineffective leadership that "failed to fulfill the implicit contract to do whatever is possible to ensure the safety of the crew."[11] The report went on to state, "Management techniques in NASA discouraged dissenting views on safety issues and ultimately created 'blind spots' about the risk to the space shuttle of the foam insulation impact." Culture's power, while often relegated to a distinction of being soft and nebulous, is, in this instance, a case of life and death. So the next time someone says that shaping the culture is not the "hard stuff" of business, remember the example of NASA and how significant the culture was in the results achieved.

Culture is the social energy built over time that can move people to act or impede them from acting. Both research and practical experience show that employees who feel connected to the culture of their organization are more productive, and nowhere does the power of leadership intention show up more than in the culture that gets shaped in an organization. An organization's behavior ripples out from the individuals leading the organization and shapes a company's identity, its values, and the results that can be achieved. The CLEAR model (fig. 25.1) is what I use when working with companies to intentionally shape their organizational cultures. We start with the strategic plan and determine what kind of culture is needed to drive the success of the business strategy. Once the cultural tenets have been determined, one or two actions for each quadrant are identified and consistently delivered. Let's examine the model to see how it works.

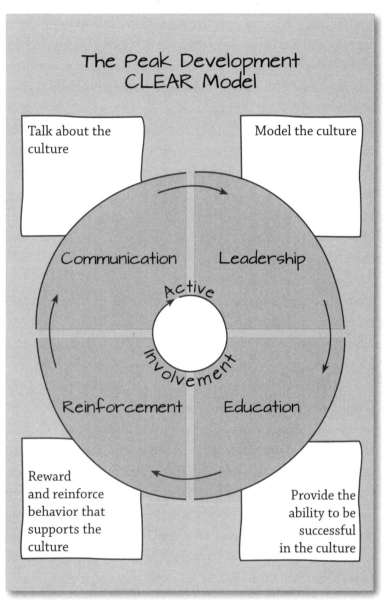

FIGURE 25.1 The Peak Development CLEAR Model

The communication quadrant includes talking about the culture, determining the right cadence, methods, and messaging, and providing venues for as many people as possible to be engaged with generating ideas to make the culture come to life. The leadership quadrant is the powerhouse quadrant of the model because the number one way culture gets shaped is by what leaders model. Identifying leaders at all levels who do and do not exemplify the desired culture allows you to leverage or coach individual leadership performance. The education quadrant focuses on providing the skills to be successful in the culture. As an example, if one of the cultural tenets is to "put the customer at the center of our business," make sure to provide education, tools, and tips on how someone would do this in practical terms. Finally, the reinforcement quadrant is about the formal and informal systems for rewarding behaviors that support the desired culture. We gravitate toward actions for which we are reinforced and away from those for which we are not. This behavior is powerful but often unconscious. In the majority of organizations, the most visible form of this is the performance management system, but remember that this is only one mechanism. Make sure to look for ways to reinforce desired behaviors throughout the year so that you will accelerate the integration of the culture into the way people are behaving. Intention underpins all of these quadrants and requires the same level of rigor and discipline that bringing a product to market demands. These four basic elements are the same whether you are shaping a culture among fifteen members of a team or fifteen thousand members of a larger organization. At the center of these elements is your active involvement, which requires commitment, passion, follow-through, marketing, charisma, a sense of urgency, patience, and more.

A consumer products company I worked with wanted to improve the way its products flowed from research to market. The motive for the project was hardly altruistic: the company was hemorrhaging. For the five years prior the company had missed its numbers (top line, bottom line, or both) and needed to do something significant to remedy the situation. Several areas of opportunity existed: accelerating innovations, driving a larger volume of product out the door, and improving overall efficiency. We actively engaged the organization in finding its own solutions, working on cross-functional teams to think about not only their piece of the company but the impact of their actions across the entire value chain.

One of the most profound suggestions was that they should change the company's culture instead of its organization chart. In similar situations I have seen organizations make the exact opposite choice, thinking that moving lines and boxes on a piece of paper would change the company. To truly change an organization, you need to pay attention to the white space between the organization's boxes: the culture in which people work. To reiterate, intentionally shaping an organization's culture takes communication, leadership, education, and reinforcement. This company realized the difference and went squarely about shaping the culture anew, implementing cross-functional teams and goals, and streamlining its efficiency. To this day the company counts that work as a cornerstone of what got it back on the right track.

Culture is formed by invitation, not mandate; by commitment, not coercion. It's about how people choose to behave, and choice makes a world of difference in the energy that gets generated. Culture is not a program that gets implemented; it is built through everyday actions and messaging. I once met an executive who believed you could build a full-scale culture plan in two ten-minute workshops. While he was being a bit hyperbolic, the essence of his point was that shaping culture does not, and in fact should not, be about grand programs. Here was his design:

- *Workshop 1*—Answer the following question: "What is standing in the way of you meeting or exceeding customer desires?" Stop doing that.

- *Workshop 2*—Answer the following question: "What are the behaviors needed for the future success of the business?" All leaders model those; get rid of leaders who don't; and reward people who exemplify them.

At all levels, we touch our organizations every day in so many ways, and leaders, especially, often have impact beyond what they are aware of. Choose to intentionally shape the culture of your organization because once you witness the power of culture, it becomes one of the most important levers of success you will ever experience.

The number one way culture is shaped is by what leaders model.

CHAPTER 26

Starting in a New Job

Every new job offers a chance to shape perception. Even if you are taking a new job within the same organization, you have the opportunity to create a story anew. Your verbal and nonverbal behavior sets the tone for your leadership from the moment you accept a new position; be deliberate about what you want that tone to be. It requires a conscious effort on your part to determine how and where you will spend your time and energy. As a leader, you have three key levers for performance:

- How you use your financial resources
- How you use your human resources
- How you use your self and your time

Guess which one gets the least amount of focus? If you guessed the last one, you guessed correctly.

The Transition Triangle (fig. 26.1) is a result of over twenty-five years of experience helping leaders transition into new roles. It illustrates five key elements of attention during a leader's transition and is a road map for determining how best to use his or her time and energy. In my

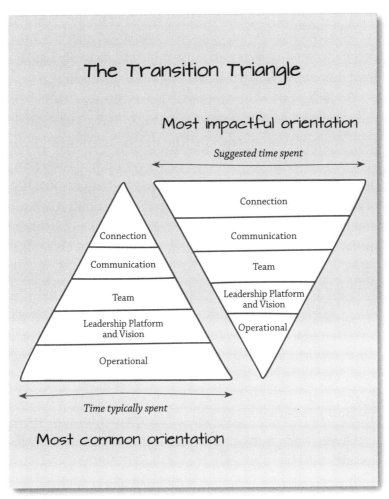

FIGURE 26.1 The Transition Triangle

experience, most leaders orient like the triangle on the left, focusing on the operational aspects—the day-to-day delivery and execution—because they have been rewarded for *what they have gotten done* in their careers and not as much for *who they were being*. However, focusing too much time on operational aspects early in a transition actually has the least amount of impact on moving the organization.

So let's start with the most impactful way to orient during times of leadership transition. Early in a transition, communication and creating a sense of connection to you—as both a person and a leader—are more critical than operational execution, as they allow you to galvanize the organization and build momentum. Everyday interactions impact the bottom line in ways both powerful and surprising. A key component of powerful leadership is the sense of connection leaders create with others, whether or not they are perceived as present, genuine, trustworthy, and inspiring. As the feeling of connection is shaped through a series of interactions, these interactions become a leader's currency; there is no more important time than during a leadership transition to pay attention to this currency. Leaders must *actively* manage their presence in *every* interaction, both formal and informal. It is a lot of work and takes a great deal of energy but it is well worth the investment.

The organization must get to know you and your priorities quickly. Clarity inspires confidence and confidence inspires commitment. In the absence of accurate information, people will fill in the blanks with their own—often negative—assumptions. Remember, communication is not a department. Communicating frequently and proactively allows you to stay ahead of the news cycle. Also remember that communication is a two-way street. Listen as much as you talk; pay attention to *how* you are listening, how present you are to others when they speak, and what tone you are setting for the conversation. Do all of this intentionally because, as we are social animals, at some level we react consciously or subconsciously to social cues. The social cues you send in the early days of a transition are critical for the results you can hope to achieve over the longer term. They will create the story of the kind of leader you are—and not some kind of clinical definition of your leadership but the qualitative, emotional element of your leadership.

In the middle of the triangle are the elements of creating your strategic platform and vision and building a strong team. Having a clear direction in your own mind about where you want to take the organization is important, but equally important is the willingness to hear the perspectives of others who have the context for the organization you are now leading. Doing so validates the experience of others who ultimately can help shape a stronger platform and vision.

It may take some time to determine whether your team members can deliver on the vision and coalesce as a high-functioning group, but remember, you are only as strong as the people that you place around you. Let them understand where you want to go and, provided they have the capability, let them make their own decisions about whether they want to join you in that direction; it doesn't have to be a love fest, there just needs to be healthy respect.

Determining whether you have the right people to deliver on the strategic platform and vision should be a key point of attention within the first quarter of your tenure.

At the bottom of the triangle are operational elements. This is where credibility gets built day in, day out. And, while it is placed at the bottom of the triangle, this does not suggest that operational execution is less important; the placement is more about the amount of time that the leader should be spending in this area. Many leaders get bogged down in day-to-day tactical elements and do not quickly establish a vision for the future or build the strong connections that create organizational success. This is a matter of focus. It is important for all leaders, but especially for those in new roles, to choose deliberately how they will spend their time and energy and create a balance that best serves them and their organization.

> ··········· GREAT IDEA ···········
>
> *Unsure of how your use of time compares with the Transition Triangle? Conduct a calendar audit. Look at the last two months of your calendar and categorize appointments against the dimensions in the model: tally the amount of time you're spending on each dimension. Determine if the way you are spending your time is providing your greatest return on leading the organization. If so, congratulations! If not, adjust your use of time going forward to deliberately align your use of time with your intentions.*

One final note: the model is shaped like an upright triangle to depict how leaders most often spend their time during a transition. They spend more time on the activities at the widest part of the base and less time on those at the tip. However, given your context you may be best served by a square, diamond, or some other shape representing how to spend your time. The bottom line is that no matter what shape fits your particular context, you should choose it intentionally and focus your time and energy accordingly.

———————

Every action or perceived inaction
shapes credibility.

———————

CHAPTER 27

Leading a Team

Think of the best team you've been a member of; now think of the individual who led the team. How did she behave? What was her contribution to making the team great? What qualities did she bring to her leadership? Now think of yourself and the teams that you currently lead or have led; how would your team members answer those three questions about you?

In the early 1980s, Margaret Mead said, "Never doubt that a small group of thoughtful, committed people can change the world. Indeed, it is the only thing that ever has." Although she wasn't referencing corporate teams per se, few forces are more powerful than those special teams that actively engage in their work together and align around a common goal. But how do you create this capacity in a team? What do you intentionally need to do to create, foster, and lead teams such as this?

We are inherently social beings shaped by those around us and by the environment in which we live. We learn from each other; we affect each other. We strive to establish a sense of belonging within the relationships, families, teams, organizations, and, on a larger scale, the cultures in which we operate. And while the topics of group dynamics, building teams, and steps to team effectiveness are the subjects of countless books in both the research and popular press, it is an unmitigated fact that the leader of any team truly shapes the tone, results, and experience of the team. Leading a team is a place of obligation and privilege. Do you treat it as such?

Leading a team with intention has three primary and symbiotic levers: trust (in you and one another), a compelling purpose, and a plan for the team's continued growth. Let's take a deeper look at each one:

- *Trust*—Trust is an inescapable success factor of great teams and is about how *real* individuals are willing to be and how safe they feel to say what's on their mind. Yet, how people develop trust is very personal and unique to each member of a team. As the leader you must ask yourself, "What am I intentionally doing to engender trust in me and among team members? How can I inspire confidence in our relationships with one another?" The fastest way to develop trust is to do what you say you are going to do, to follow through on commitments. How are you making this part of the culture of the team and what are you modeling in your behavior around keeping commitments and following through? Remember that the number one way culture gets shaped is by what leaders model; to lead a team whose members trust one another requires constant awareness of what you are modeling.

- *A Compelling Purpose*—Think of a time when you were part of something where the purpose or vision was so compelling that you felt inspired by it, moved by it, absorbed by it. It made you walk down the hall in a different way, occupied your thoughts, and created the possibility to be part of something bigger than yourself. Think about the vision or purpose of the team you are currently leading; does it have this fire, this energy? If not, why not? If so, bravo!

- *The Team's Continued Growth*—I often bristle at well-intentioned but misguided approaches to developing teams—the one-day team-building events or the meeting designs that have team building carved out as a stand-alone agenda item. While these are approaches that most leaders have some experience and comfort with, the reality is that the highest performing teams know that the secret is about investing in the team's growth regularly, not episodically. They know that mastery requires practice. Look at professional sports teams or world-class orchestras. They meet regularly to refine how they work together. In the business world, however, it's often assumed that teams will simply develop on their own, perhaps after an initial team kickoff. The reality is that often they don't get the investment over time that helps them reach their fullest potential. Development that is conducted over a sustained period of time allows team members the opportunity to reflect upon and change their behavior. As adults, we learn by doing and we change by experiencing. Shifting

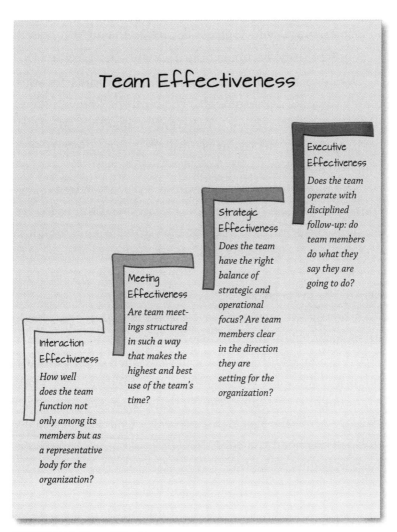

FIGURE 27.1 Team Effectiveness

one's behavior—and even more challenging, a team's behavior—is a process, not an event. Designing team development that simultaneously advances the team's business and leadership goals creates the highest return on investment.

While each team is unique, a model to consider for your team's ongoing development focuses on the following four dimensions: interaction effectiveness, meeting effectiveness, strategic effectiveness, and execution effectiveness (fig. 27.1).

All four are equally important and are interrelated. This framework allows room for great customization; there are no right and wrong answers for how teams should organize and structure themselves and their processes. The goal is about finding the solutions that best meet the team and the organization's needs.

I have seen teams move mountains under tight deadlines and demanding conditions. What made these feats possible was an intentional leader, a sense of pride in the team, and a respect for the unique contribution each member brought to the table. These are not team characteristics that are achieved overnight, nor without deliberate focus. And, as has been the core theme of this book, the team's success begins with you.

Organizations cannot mandate trust;
it must be earned.

CHAPTER 28

Working Globally

In January 1993, I arrived in Paris for a two-year expatriate assignment. At the time, I spoke exactly three words of French. I had every desire to learn the language before transferring, but the time between getting the job and moving to Europe was short and allowed little time to work on my language skills. About two or three months into my new job, I was working through a difficult employee-relations issue. The person at the center of that issue came to speak with me; I watched how hard it was for her to try to find words in English to explain the essence of the situation and I felt that it was very unfair to her. Here I was in her country, it was a painful issue for her, and she had to speak in her second language. Language matters: it is the quickest access to the cognitive part of our brain and shapes opinion and possible outcomes. That evening I bought books, tapes, and a television in order to immerse myself in the language and become fluent.

About seven or eight months into the assignment, I had another similar issue, this time with a gentleman who came in and started to speak in very stilted English, not knowing if I was capable of understanding him in French. I said, "No, it's okay. Feel free to speak with me in French." He did and the difference in terms of his ease and how expediently we could get to the heart of the matter and resolve the issue was huge. He was able to articulate—in a language that he could connect with—exactly what the issue was. Language matters.

On that same assignment, I was visiting the home of an English couple that was living and working in Paris—let's call them Kate and Jonathan. They had invited me to dinner to meet Kate's mother, who was visiting from the United Kingdom. As we sat around the table, Kate's mother asked, "So Mindy, have you done any shopping while you've been in Paris?"

"Not really," I said. "I've just bought a couple pairs of pants and a few scarves."

She looked appalled at my answer and I was unsure why. I had absolutely no idea what had just transpired. Kate excused herself to make coffee and invited me to join her. When we got into the kitchen, she burst out laughing.

"What just happened?" I asked. "Why are you laughing?"

"You just told my mother you bought undergarments."

I hadn't been aware that what Americans call "pants" the British call "slacks" or "trousers." To the British, "pants" means "undergarments." As a proper Englishwoman, her mother had been offended that I'd been so personal with her since we'd only just met. Even with what I'd assumed was the same language, my words had landed differently than I'd intended because of the difference in our cultures.

While those examples highlight the language challenges that can ensue around the globe, cultural differences take many forms. For example, relationship to time, power, and hierarchy; approach to discussion and debate; and general work styles. Obviously others could be added, but these provide food for thought in considering how different the lens could be depending on the culture you are starting from. While we must be careful not to make sweeping generalizations about other cultures, differences must be taken into consideration from country to country and region to region. An approach that works in North America may not work in Asia. What makes sense in Europe may not in Africa. I will say, however, that I have tested the concept of "being intentional" in Europe, Asia, Africa, and America, and have found it to resonate across all of those geographies.

Accept where others are starting from: don't judge it. Figure out how to meet their needs before you meet your own. You may need to approach situations differently than you are accustomed to, but you will build stronger relationships and create better business results.

The world gets smaller with each passing year.

THE RIPPLE EFFECT
Paying It Forward

In part I, we looked at the three layers of growth: awareness, integration, and embodiment. In part V, we focus on embodiment, wherein the new skills and behavior you've learned become an integral part of the way you function. Getting there requires consistency over time, so we'll consider ways to incorporate this new way of thinking into your work.

Embodiment also implies that you are serving as an example to others. I urge you to make it personal. Be the pebble in the pond that starts a ripple, and find ways to encourage others in your organization and in the world around you to lead with intention.

*Until one is committed, there is hesitancy,
the chance to turn back, always ineffectiveness . . .
Whatever you can do or dream you can, begin it;
boldness has genius, power and magic in it.
Begin it now.*

GOETHE

Making It Personal

All leadership is personal. No platitudes of leadership theory can gloss over the inevitable fact that it boils down to you and your decision to be intentional in your leadership. You can be successful without being intentional in your leadership; it happens all the time. However, success without intention is short-lived. Great leaders take seriously their privilege and their obligation to affect others' lives. Great leaders realize that they can trigger so much simply by how they behave. Great leaders operate intentionally. It is a choice and a decision.

A few months ago I watched a senior team listening to a CEO and his top executives talk about the need to elevate leadership ability in the organization. As I looked around I saw eyes glazed over, with about one-third of the audience not really listening and a drone of corporate "blah-blah-speak" permeating the room. I wondered why the leaders didn't see the nonverbal cues in the audience and adjust their approach. Why had they not been more intentional about how they engaged people, particularly given the topic of the talk? They would have been so much more effective if they had shared stories of their own leadership journeys. It would have made the exchange more personal, more human, and created a deeper sense of connection in the room. An opportunity for bigger impact was lost; this happens every day, over and over again in our organizations. Own the impact you are having. Make it personal. Be more intentional.

Make intentionality part of your leadership platform. When something isn't happening the way you want it to, don't look outside of yourself—look at yourself. It is not acceptable, as a leader, to be a passenger. Lead. Take responsibility. How many times have you been in a meeting and heard people in the room mumbling under their breath about their disagreement with what is being said? Or, perhaps, mumbled under your own breath? Great leaders do not mumble under their breath. They don't stand outside of the problem complaining about it. They own making things better. They embrace the privilege and the obligation of what being a leader means. They make it personal.

All leadership is personal.

Being a Pebble in the Pond

··

One of the greatest pleasures of my work is when I hear someone with whom I've worked using phrases or concepts that I've shared with them or witness them helping others be more intentional. I feel as though I've tossed a pebble in a pond, causing ripples to spread far beyond the point of entry. A grand vision plays in my mind: that the simple practice of being self-aware and more intentional has the capacity for impact on a substantial scale.

Case in point: I'd been working with a client for many years when she was named vice president of human resources—her first time holding a vice president title. She decided, going in, that she wanted to create an organization where people truly felt that it mattered that they came to work, so she started looking for opportunities for the leaders to model how much they valued the employees. She didn't need to look far. One of the first projects proposed to her was the redesign of the organization's operating model. Traditionally with this kind of work, companies bring in external consultants to tell them how they should be operating. She realized that this conventional approach would run counter to what she was trying to create; it would send a message that the company needed to be told how to improve the way it operated.

She asked for my advice on how this work could be done differently and we worked together to create an approach that engaged the internal leaders in redesigning the operating model themselves. It was a bold and risky proposition as it would put the power and responsibility squarely in the hands of the internal teams working on the project. She sold the idea to the president and his executive team and we got started. She personally modeled her belief that the organization had all the tools needed and that the executive team needed to trust them—even when it was a little scary. These were high stakes for sure—for her, the employees, the organization, and the executive team. Her behavior was the bedrock that made it possible; her belief that it was possible is what made it possible. What this approach did for the people inside the organization—the fact that the executive team believed that the team members on the project had the answers and wanted to hear their recommendations—was palpable. One executive came to the initial launch meeting questioning the value of this project; he approached it with great cynicism and a "this too shall pass" mentality. At the final approval meeting, a little over one hundred days from the project's launch, when the meeting was just getting ready to close, this same executive

> •••••••• GREAT IDEA ••••••••
> *Think of someone in your career who made you better at what you do. Have you let them know? How could you have a similar impact on someone else?*

stood up and asked if he could speak. I held my breath. The vice president of human resources held her breath. We both hoped that all the good work that had gone into creating a lasting and profound impact on the organization would not be diminished by what he was about to say. When he began speaking, it became clear the work had made a deep impression on him. He said, "We created a great operating model for the business, but that hasn't mattered as much to me as what I've gained personally working with my colleagues. I can't begin to explain how much I've gotten out of what it took to get here; how much it's meant that we've been able to do this work together and have the leadership believe in us. For the first time in a long time, I feel like my voice matters." You could have heard a pin drop in the room. It was the capstone on a profoundly important project for many of the people in the room, me included. All because one person, the vice president of human resources, decided to be a pebble in the pond, creating ripples that had long-lasting impact.

Choose to be a pebble in the pond versus a grain in the sand. Choose to create those ripples through others. Decide to make a difference. Be a catalyst for unleashing potential in yourself, others, and the world.

Be a pebble in the pond.

Growing Intentionality in Future Leaders

We live in a fast-paced, constantly evolving world. Research and innovation bring new products; mergers and acquisitions expand reach; and intense competition causes companies to rethink their business models, strategies, and approaches. Developing leaders who can succeed in this challenging landscape requires learning beyond the classic cookie cutter, one-size-fits-all approach. We must move beyond programmatic, classroom-based models to more customized development that emphasizes real-life challenges and real-time feedback. Just as leaders must evolve and grow in how they lead, methods of developing leaders require equal change and growth. As an example, the design of a high potential academy that we created with one of our clients emphasized narrative feedback, high-risk issues that needed to be solved, one-on-one time with senior executives, and ongoing cohort learning and peer mentorship with fellow attendees.

While skills such as self-awareness, intention, and adaptability have historically been characterized as "nice to do" skills, they are essential for today's leaders and should be considered foundational for success. In my experience it is a rare executive development program that sees development of these skills as foundational for a leader's success. While many of these programs incorporate 360-degree feedback into their designs—asking the people who work most closely with an individual, whether superior, peer, or subordinate, to provide feedback on his or her performance—they usually stop at a debrief of the resulting data and an action plan for addressing a few key areas. This is not enough. Developing skills of awareness and intention requires the weaving of those skills into every element of a development program. As an example, for more than a decade I have run a program that builds organization development (OD) skills in human resource practitioners. While it is centered on providing practical tools to deepen OD skills, the most important thing taught is that participants are their own best tool and that highly effective practitioners know how to use themselves intentionally. The same is true for all leaders, no matter the functional areas in which they work.

Back in the mid-'90s, I met with the senior leaders of a company that was young, innovative, exciting, and fast-paced; we had worked together previously on developing a corporate university, and they were interested in taking that approach to the next level and accelerating the development of the leaders in the organization. The company was growing rapidly and it needed leaders who could keep up with the challenges. When the university was conceived a couple of years prior, it had the active support of the senior leadership; the CEO and several vice presidents even functioned as faculty. As a result, it was highly regarded. The company's employees competed for admission, and the sessions were praised as practical and engaging.

However, within just a couple of years of its inception, business priorities competed for the executives' time, the offerings began to feel stagnant, and the proverbial "wheels on the wagon" began to wobble. At a meeting where we were discussing a major reinvestment in the program and the value of the important outcomes and relationships that had resulted from the initial investment, I stated, "It comes down to this: organizations grow when people grow, and people grow when they invest and are invested in."

One final note about growing awareness and intentionality in future leaders: organizations do not come close to considering these kinds of skills equally with functional expertise when promoting leaders and creating succession plans, and therefore reinforce a model of behavior that will have limited value in the organizations of the future. We must get serious about the need for congruency between what we know the best leaders exemplify and what often gets developed and rewarded. For the last decade, and even more so in the last five years, developing leadership talent has shown up on corporate objectives over and over again, but few companies have seen significant progress toward this objective. Why is this the case? What we are reinforced for doing, we will do. Simply put, leaders are not reinforced for developing leaders. By creating norms that make the development of other leaders an essential part of being a successful executive, we will see the tide turn.

Organizations grow when people grow.

Keeping It Going

I once knew a leader who, whenever anyone returned from a development opportunity, would take the individual for a walk and ask, "What did you learn?" Answering this question required employees to reflect on their learning and put it into a coherent context, cementing the experience. This simple practice cost the company nothing, but the leaders estimated that it increased the retention rate of development opportunities by three to five times. A biological basis exists for this phenomenon. As we discussed earlier regarding recent research in neuroscience, the amount of attention given to a new insight determines how well it is retained. Each time our focus is drawn to a specific idea, we literally strengthen a circuit in our brain. With enough attention, these circuits become permanent, intrinsic parts of our thinking. The same is true for leading intentionally: simply knowing the concept will cause you to pay more attention to it and with enough attention, it will become part of the way you think and operate. You can strengthen the connections by more frequently drawing your attention to the topic. Challenge yourself to use one or more of the tools in this book on a weekly basis. Answer the eight questions in chapter 8 quarterly or yearly.

Albert Einstein said, "No problem can be solved from the same consciousness that created it; we must learn to see the world anew." Make this your challenge: to see your leadership anew, move away from conventional wisdom that may be simply conventional but not wisdom, and challenge yourself to be persistent in your quest to lead with intention.

People who understand what this book is suggesting and put it into practice have turned around whole companies, realized the financial results that all organizations want, and created growth possibilities for individuals beyond what those individuals dreamed possible. They've created energy in their organizations that people want to be part of. They haven't exclusively focused on how to squeeze more money out of a process or how to sell more products or how to have more efficient cycle times. They started with these questions: where do we want to go, what's our plan, who's my leadership team, and how are we getting everybody's energy and voice in the process to pull off the plan? And the results have followed. In this cynical day and age, it takes time for people to believe, but start today, consistently lead with intention, and the money will always follow.

Choose.

CHAPTER 33

Being Intentional in Your Life Outside of Work

When you commit to a new possibility, it alters who you are; when you take a stand, it transforms how you behave. Imagine, if you will, living in a future in which the vast majority of people are mindful of their impact, intentional about how they show up, and conscious of the choices they make about their behavior. How differently would our world operate? Imagine this concept beyond your professional life; imagine it being alive in your family, with your friends, and out in the world. Here are a few examples I've witnessed that illustrate these ideas in life outside of work:

- A mother and father who were out to dinner with their two teenage children and actively engaged with them throughout the meal. Their presence was impressive and signaled to the teens that they were valued, worth listening to, and respected.

- A woman who delivered a tin of cookies to the firefighters at our local fire station to say thank you for what they do, making an intentional gesture to ensure they knew they were appreciated.

- Wawa, a popular convenience store on the East Coast where patrons hold doors open for each other with a consistency I have never experienced elsewhere. I must admit to not knowing how the company cultivated this behavior in its patrons, but no matter which Wawa I stop in, there is a civility present that I so appreciate. It is as if the culture of Wawa has dictated this level of intention and kindness.

- The positive impact of a cashier at a crowded airport restaurant greeting me with a smile and a "How is your day going?" when cashiers at other shops were making less positive choices, most likely out of habit rather than out of intention.

The choices people made in these examples matter. Making a difference costs nothing but awareness and choice and could create a groundswell in how we see each other and treat each other. Imagine members of the US Congress looking at themselves in this way, examining their behavior behind the lens of the impact it is having, consciously choosing to look for the win-win versus the win-lose. Utopia? I don't think so. Choice. I said at the beginning of the book that I had a grand vision of the possibilities that flow from people being intentional in their lives, professionally and personally. I remain steadfastly convinced that being intentional can change the world, and I think this world could use a bit of changing.

Create an intentional world.

Closing Thoughts

In the confrontation between
the stream and the rock, the stream
always wins . . . not through strength,
but through persistence.

NATIVE AMERICAN SAYING

An idea without action is simply an idea. I hope as you've reached this page of the book you are ready to be intentional in your life. Don't assume it's just going to happen; create a plan, work the muscle, and notice the results. Answer the following questions to create your Be Intentional Plan:

1. One thing that really struck me in this book was . . .

2. One action I will take to be a more intentional leader is . . .

3. One way I will track my progress is . . .

4. One person I will discuss this with is . . .

5. One concept I will pass along to others is . . .

Finally, here's a list of the "top five reminders" related to each section of the book to jump-start your journey of leading with intention.

- Recognizing your impact:
  - In all of your life, you are the critical success factor. Outcomes achieved depend on your awareness—of your impact, others, the context in which you are operating, and the goals you are trying to achieve.
  - How aware are you of how you're perceived?
  - Every action has an impact; choose wisely the impact you want to have.
  - One person truly can make a difference.
  - How have you chosen to behave today?
- Leading with intention:
  - You are 100 percent responsible for the tone you set.
  - Shape your mind-sets or your mind-sets will shape you.
  - Actions speak louder than words.
  - Clarity inspires confidence and confidence inspires commitment.
  - Do you do what you say you are going to do?
- Being intentional in your communication:
  - Be present—verbally and nonverbally. Pay attention to how you are listening.
  - If people feel heard, they feel valued.

- Good work doesn't speak for itself; you have to speak for your good work.
- Never being afraid is unrealistic; learning to be brave is invaluable.
- If you are willing to stay in a conversation long enough to truly hear another, you can achieve anything.
- Impacting your organization:
  - People want it to matter that they came to work.
  - The number one way culture is shaped is by what leaders model.
  - Every action or perceived inaction shapes credibility.
  - How do you impact the culture and tone of the organization? How does the culture and tone impact you?
  - The world gets smaller with each passing year.
- Paying it forward:
  - All leadership is personal.
  - Be a pebble in the pond.
  - Organizations grow when people grow.
  - Choose.
  - Create an intentional world.

Additional Resources

Continue your learning with these additional resources:

- *The Leading with Intention Assessment*—Find out how intentional you are with this free online assessment tool. This quick survey measures your level of intention and offers suggestions for becoming more aware of your impact and more present in your leadership. Get started at leadingwithintentionbook.com.

- *The Leading with Intention Discussion Guide*—Talking about the book is a great way to begin integrating its concepts into your leadership. Conversation requires people to reflect on their learning and put it into a coherent context, cementing the experience. Use the discussion guide to keep the conversation going within your team, book club, or leadership development program. To download the guide, visit leadingwithintentionbook.com and click on "Additional Resources."

- *Peak Development Radio*—This podcast features great conversations and practical advice for making your organization stronger. Each month, host Dr. Mindy Hall talks with current business leaders about the issues and opportunities they face and the lessons they can share. Past guests have included leaders from Johnson & Johnson, Starbucks, Novartis, Pfizer, Biogen Idec, and more. Episodes are available on iTunes, through Stitcher radio on demand, or at peakdevelopment.com/radio.

- *Growing Your Organization*—This blog emphasizes that all organizations—from start-ups to Fortune 50 multinationals—must continue to grow or they will perish. But growth isn't solely about size; it encompasses culture, strategy, innovation, efficiency, leadership, teamwork, and more. Dr. Mindy Hall offers new perspectives on topics that impact the growth of your enterprise and your workforce. Challenge your thinking at peakdevelopment.com/blog.

- *Peak Development's Article Review Service*—This free monthly service combs through over two dozen magazines, journals, websites, and blogs to bring you the best reading on culture, leadership, teams, and more. We do the legwork so you can do the learning. Follow us on Facebook (Peak Development Consulting, LLC) or Twitter (@PeakDevConsult) to be notified of new articles as we discover them. Or receive our convenient monthly e-mail with links to the top five to seven articles by registering at peakdevelopment.com.

Notes

Chapter 5

1. R. E. Petty and P. Brinol, "Psychological Processes Underlying Persuasion: A Social Psychological Approach," *Diogenes* 55, no. 1 (2008): 52–67.

Chapter 11

2. D. Rock and J. Schwartz, "The Neuroscience of Leadership," *Strategy+Business*, no. 43 (Summer 2006): 71–79.

3. T. Koyama et al., "The Subjective Experience of Pain: Where Expectation Becomes Reality," *Proceedings of the National Academy of Sciences* 102, no. 36 (September 6, 2005): 12950–12955.

4. Rock and Schwartz, "Neuroscience of Leadership."

5. J. M. Schwartz, H. P. Stapp, and M. Beauregard, "Quantum Physics in Neuroscience and Psychology: A Neurophysical Model of the Mind-Brain Interaction," *Philosophical Transactions of the Royal Society B* 360, no. 1458 (June 29, 2005): 1309–1327.

6. J. Gillham et al., "Prevention of Depressive Symptoms in Schoolchildren: Two-Year Follow-Up," *Psychological Science* 6, no. 6 (1995): 343–351. L. Jaycox et al., "Prevention of Depressive Symptoms in

Schoolchildren," *Behavior Research and Therapy* 32 (1994): 801–816.

7. G. Olivero, K. D. Bane, and R. E. Kopelman, "Executive Coaching as a Transfer of Training Tool: Effects on Productivity in a Public Agency," *Public Personnel Management* 26, no. 4 (Winter 1997): 461–469.

Chapter 12

8. L. Wilson and H. Wilson, *Play to Win! Choosing Growth over Fear in Work and Life* (Austin: Bard Press, 1998), 69.

Chapter 17

9. A. Mehrabian and M. Wiener, "Decoding of Inconsistent Communications," *Journal of Personality and Social Psychology* 6, no. 1 (May 1967): 109–114.

Chapter 23

10. J. Connolly et al., "Human fMRI Evidence for the Neural Correlates of Preparatory Set," *Nature Neuroscience* 5, no. 12 (2002): 1345–1352.

Chapter 25

11. Columbia Accident Investigation Board, *Report Volume I* (Washington DC: National Aeronautics and Space Administration and the Government Printing Office, 2003), 170.

Index

....

A

actions
  ideas without, 127–129
  interpretation of, 22–23
  showing intentions in,
    21–22
active listening, 62
adversaries, 73
Agreement-Trust Matrix, 70–73
allies, 71
appearance, impact of your,
  10–11, 63
approach to others. *See*
  communication
Argyris, Chris, 44
articulating a compelling
  purpose, 17
assessing the context, 17
assumptions, impact of mind-
  sets on, 43
attention
  draws on, 14
  to ideas or mind-sets, 41
  from others, 14
  retention and, 123–124

attention density, 40–41
awareness, 3–4, 5
  as controllable variable, 9
  of mind-sets, 41, 42, 43–44
  moment-to-moment, 12
awareness layer of growth, 4

B

Bannister, Roger, 39–40
behavior
  and creating an
    environment, 31
  effects of, 51, 118
  impact of intentionality, 15
  leading with, 21–22
  moving from cognition to,
    4, 5
  others' perceptions of
    leaders', 54
  reinforcing others', 25, 95
  team's, 108
  unintentional impact of, xiv
behavioral change, steps in, 4–6
Being and Doing model, 87, 88
Be Intentional Plan, 127–129

engagement
  dimensions of, 70–71
  of informal leaders, 20
environment, 31–35, 47–48
executive effectiveness, 107
expectations
  reality shaped by, 40
  for successful leadership, 86
experiences
  identifying and having new,
    50
  mind-sets informed by, 42
expertise, functional 86–88

F
facial expression, 62, 63
fear, 22–23, 77
feedback
  asking for, 71
  skills for giving, 121
55/38/7 rule, 62, 64
focus
  effect on brain of, 40
  improving, 19
  during transition to new job,
    100, 102
following through, 51–52
foreign language challenges,
    109–111
formal leadership style, 22–23
functional expertise, 86–88

G
gestures, 63
growth
  layers of, 3–6
  of organizations, 122
  team's continued, 106, 108

H
"hanging in the air" metaphor,
    77–78
hyperconnectivity, 54–55

I
ideas
  attention to, 41
  focusing, 19
  using mind mapping for,
    48–50
  without actions, 127–129
identity, shaping of, 40–41
impact
  awareness of your, 61–65,
    128
  choosing your, 13
  of context, 81–82
  on environment, 33
  examples of, 89–91
  gap between intent and, 8–9
  of level of intention, xiii
  making a difference through,
    16–17
  matching intention with,
    21–26
  of mind-set on assumptions,
    43
  of others on you, 31–32
  recognizing your, 7–8
  reflecting on making your, 57
  of shared vision, 89
  unintentional, of behavior,
    xii
  of verbal and nonverbal
    communication, 61–65
  of your appearance, 10–11,
    63
  on your organization, 129

Acknowledgments

Thank you for choosing this book to read. As I know that time is precious, I appreciate that you are spending some of yours with my words. My greatest hope is that they will inspire you and move you to action.

To Teri and Paul, who, amidst your very busy schedules, provided great feedback and ideas, thank you. To Sharon, who offered counsel and guidance, this book is better because of your involvement. And to Greg, a heartfelt thanks for all you have done to bring this book to life; it truly would not have been possible without you.

Finally, to Robin, whose steadfast belief in both me and this book's message has made all the difference, thank you from the bottom of my heart.

About the Author

Mindy Hall, PhD, is the president and CEO of Peak Development Consulting, LLC. Since founding the company in 1996, she has worked with clients throughout North America, Europe, Africa, and Asia to create sustainable organization and leadership development solutions: helping leaders create solutions for today's challenges while growing their capacity to lead future endeavors from within. Clients include leading pharmaceutical, biotechnology, technology, insurance, manufacturing, government, and nonprofit organizations, several of which are among the Fortune 50.

Mindy has over twenty-five years of experience in organization and leadership development. Her early corporate career spanned positions in the pharmaceutical and banking industries, including experience in global roles and as an expatriate in Paris. She began her career as the director of a nonprofit twenty-four-hour crisis center and has always been surprised how transferrable the skills were from crisis center to corporate work.

She holds a doctorate in human and organizational systems from Fielding Graduate University, and her doctoral dissertation, "Deep Learning: A Case Study Exploration," was published in paperback in 2011. She also holds master's degrees in both organization development and human resources management.

Mindy hosts the podcast *Peak Development Radio*, featuring great conversations and practical advice for making your organization stronger. Guests have included leaders from Johnson & Johnson, Starbucks, Novartis, Pfizer, Biogen Idec, and more. Episodes are available through peakdevelopment.com, Stitcher radio on demand, and iTunes.

She counts herself fortunate to be doing work she loves with people she respects. Her philosophy can be summed up in eight simple words: "I want it to matter that we met."

To connect with Mindy, visit drmindyhall.com, or follow her on Facebook or Twitter.

About Peak Development Consulting, LLC

Stronger, more capable organizations. Leaders who inspire. Teams that are greater than the sum of their parts. Over our nearly two decades of experience, these are just a few of the results Peak Development has achieved with clients.

Our full suite of custom organization and leadership development solutions is designed to unlock the potential and build the long-term capacity of the companies with which we work. Our clients range from Fortune 50 multinationals to entrepreneurial start-ups to nonprofits, and our work has included projects throughout North America, Europe, Africa, and Asia. Whether we are designing business models, shaping cultures, cultivating leaders, developing teams, or building HR capacity, our goal is to deliver the best solutions for our clients' unique business challenges.

What really differentiates us, though, is how we achieve results:

- We customize each engagement, tailoring an approach that drives results for your organization.

- We build capability so your organization has the knowledge and experience to sustain efforts over the long term.

- We actively involve the organization, as people will nurture what they help create.

- We focus on the system and take a multidimensional approach.

- We develop cultures, leaders, and teams.

   For more information, please visit peakdevelopment.com.